LEGAL ISSUES JOURNAL

Volume 4 Issue 2 July 2016

LEGAL ISSUES JOURNAL

Volume 4 Issue 2 July 2016

www.uklsa.co.uk/law-review

Legal Issues is an international journal managed and published by the UK Law and Society Association (UKLSA). The Journal publishes fine research in all fields of law on the basis of its contribution to the society, originality, interdisciplinary interest, and quality. *Legal Issues* also provides important news and interpretation on changes in the legal world and coming trends affecting law, lawyers, and society. The Journal has two primary aims. First, to facilitate a forum for the sharing of knowledge, news, and trends concerning the application of the law throughout the globe and for further development in all fields of law. Second, to ensure the dissemination of fine accessible work to the public throughout the world.

ISSN 2050-005X (Online)

Contents

The Dilemma of Indirect Expropriation of Host States and the Right to Regulate in the International Investment Sphere

Bashayer Al-Mukhaizeem†

This article examines the situation where a State embraces an investment belonging to a foreigner. How a State can regulate its affairs without harming foreign investors and without being accused of implied expropriation of such investment? Some municipal laws restrict the government's power to expropriate investments indirectly, such as Cambodia's Investment Act 1994.[1] *Other domestic laws do not constrain the government from doing so. This article examines specific measures in order to determine whether a State creates new legislation to disengage itself from its obligations towards foreign investment, or whether such a rule is promulgated merely to govern internal matters.*

Keywords: International Investment Law, Indirect Expropriation.

1. INTRODUCTION

In many countries, foreign investment has expanded to reach between 50-100% of all major sectors, such as railways, mining, and banking.[2] Cross-

---

† LLM, Sussex University; Legal Researcher, Civil Service Commission of Kuwait.

[1] Art 9 Cambodia Investment Act 1994. See: Lorenz Cotula, *Foreign Investment, Law and Sustainable Development: A Handbook on Agriculture and Extractive Industries* (London: International Institute for Environment and Development, 2014), 22.

[2] Ian Brownlie, *Principles of Public International Law* (Oxford University Press, 2003), 508.

border investment exceeds $1.5 trillion annually[3] and is regarded as an engine for economic prosperity, exploiting a State's productive potential[4] and providing a source of foreign skills, information, technology, expertise and foreign currency revenue.[5] In most cases, a State would not sacrifice such advantages, which are seen as outweighing any other consideration. It is undesirable for a country to receive negative publicity and potentially lose its reputation as a foreign investment venue.[6]

There is a three-part test to determine whether the transaction is to be regarded as an investment enterprise.[7] Firstly, the duration of the project should last for several years.[8] Secondly, the investment should have a vital role in generating a regular income contributing towards and promoting community affairs, such as consumer services, technology and marketing assistance.[9] Thirdly, investment activity entails a certain degree of risk associated with the difficulty of predicting the transaction's consequences.[10]

The formation of investment tribunals, such as the International Centre for Settlement of Investment Disputes (ICSID), has created an arbitral forum to resolve disputes between foreign investors and the State where the investment occurred (host State) through the incorporation of ICSID in many bilateral investment treaties (BITs).[11] BITs aim to protect and promote international investments.[12] Investment tribunals have a substantial role to play in determining whether the acts of the host State amount to indirect expropriation, or reflect the normal exercise of the State's right to regulate, in light of the facts and circumstances of each case.[13] This paper discusses the criteria used by investment tribunals to reach such a distinction.

Indirect expropriation may occur by measures that cause the value or usage of the investment to diminish considerably, even if the possession of the

---

[3] Gary Born, *International Arbitration: Law and Practice* (Netherlands: Wolters Kluwer, 2012), 411.
[4] Peter Bossche & Werner Zdouc, *The Law and Policy of the World Trade Organization* (Cambridge University Press, 2014), 20.
[5] Surya Subedi, 'International Investment Law' in Malcolm Evans, *International Law* (Oxford University Press, 2014), 741.
[6] Margaret Moses, *The Principles and Practice of International Commercial Arbitratio* (Cambridge University Press, 2012), 231.
[7] Krista Schefer, *International Investment Law* (Cheltenham: Edward Elgar Publishing, 2013), 59.
[8] Ibid., 59.
[9] Ibid., 60, 72.
[10] Ibid., 73.
[11] Alan Redfern & Martin Hunter, *Redfern and Hunter on International Arbitration* (Oxford University Press, 2009), 467.
[12] Ibid., 468, Lorenz Cotula, *op. cit.*, 21.
[13] Alan Redfern & Martin Hunter, *op. cit.,* 489.

asset remains with the investor.[14] In other words, indirect expropriation, unlike direct expropriation, does not entail a manifest taking or formal transfer of the title to the host State, but involves covert interference[15] that efficiently incapacitates the use, enjoyment or disposal of property[16] through unduly burdensome regulations.[17] The aggrieved investor should be compensated, even though he retains the formal title.[18] The Convention on the Protection of Foreign Property provides examples of indirect expropriation such as arbitrary taxation, prohibition of dismissal of staff, and refusal of access to raw materials.[19]

It was argued in the UN Conference on Trade and Development that measures which cause 'effective loss of management, use or control, or a significant depreciation of the value of the assets of a foreign investor' are considered indirect taking.[20] Some scholars notice that if the alleged measures are at the limit of regulatory activity, the affected investor will not be compensated.[21] Others argue that the harmful effect of the State's regulatory actions should be compensated even if they aim to protect the environment, culture or health.[22]

2. The Difference between Indirect Expropriation and the State's Right To Regulate

The issue is that the host State mostly broadens the concept of non-compensable actions under its sovereignty and regulatory prerogatives,[23] whereas the foreign investor will maintain that the measures appertain to

---

[14] Ibid., 497, Gary Born, *op. cit.,* 430.
[15] *Parkerings Compagniet AS v Republic of Lithuania case* (2007) Case No. ARB/05/8.
[16] *PSEG Global Inc. and Konya Ilgin Elektrik Üretim ve Ticaret Limited Sirketi v Republic of Turkey* (2007) Case No. ARB/02/5. Rudolf Dolzer & Christoph Schreuer, *Principles of International Investment Law* (Oxford University Press, 2012), 103.
[17] Gary Born, *op. cit.*, 430.
[18] Rudolf Dolzer & Christoph Schreuer, *op. cit.,* 102, Bjorn Kunoy, 'Developments in Indirect Expropriation Case Law in ICSID Transnational Arbitration' (2005) 6(3) *The Journal of World Investment & Trade*, 468-469.
[19] Anna Luca, 'Indirect Expropriations and Regulatory Takings: What Role for the "Legitimate Expectations' of Foreign Investor" in Giorgio Sacerdoti, *General Interests in International Investment Law* (Cambridge University Press, 2014), 61.
[20] Rudolf Dolzer & Christoph Schreuer, *op. cit.,* 103.
[21] Ibid., 102.
[22] Gary Born, *op. cit.,* 430.
[23] Ibid., 434.

indirect taking.[24] Making the distinction is not an easy task and needs casuistic methods.[25] There are some guided approaches, which are discussed below.

2.1.Prejudice Doctrine

According to this doctrine, the aim of the State's adoption of harmful measures is purely to damage the investor's reputation or profits, and the interests of public welfare are not pursued.[26] Let us assume that the investor produces apple juices which contain 4% sugar and then a health rule is promulgated in the host State to ban any apple juices that contain more than 3% sugar. The question therefore arises whether the law should be regarded as an intentional act of the State to impede the investor's activity. This is a controversial matter. Remarkably, a State may abuse the right to regulate by issuing arbitrary measures which harm the foreign investor, such as, sequestration, oppressive administrative proceedings,[27] generating hostility towards the foreign investor through the media,[28] and practices associated with dumping, namely importing cheaper products that cause material injury to the foreign investor who produces similar products.[29] The Permanent Court of International Justice (PCIJ) resorted to such a doctrine in order to classify host States' acts as indirect expropriation when there is not any legal justification.[30]

Noticeably, a State may appear to show concern for the public, however it is necessary to scrutinise the previous failed attempts of a State to impede investment activity. Examples, such as the postponement of issuing a license and violating contractual obligations, can appear to be deceptive. Critics assert that attempts may be made by a State to conceal surreptitious measures,[31] namely taking a crisis as an excuse to adopt measures that adversely conflict with the rights of the investors.[32]

---

[24] Rudolf Dolzer & Christoph Schreuer. *op. cit.,* 102.
[25] Bjorn Kunoy, *op. cit.,* 467.
[26] Krista Schefer, *op. cit.,* 208-209.
[27] Stephen Schwebel, *Justice in International Law* (Cambridge University Press, 1994), 387.
[28] Rudolf Dolzer & Christoph Schreuer, *op. cit.,* 99-129.
[29] Peter Bossche & Werner Zdouc, *op. cit.,* 39.
[30] Bjorn Kunoy, *op. cit.,* 470.
[31] Georg Schwarzenberger, *Foreign Investment and International Law* (London: Steven & Sons, 1969), 181.
[32] Charles Brower & Stephan Schill, 'Is Arbitration a Threat or a Boon to the Legitimacy of International Investment Law?' (2009) 9(4), *The Chicago Journal of International Law*, 483.

Nevertheless, some scholars affirm that the arbitrator should focus on the effect of the State's actions on foreign investment,[33] not tracing the State's intention to expropriate indirectly.[34] Article 10(5) of the Harvard Project for Responsibility of States for Injuries to the Economic Interests of Aliens excludes some States' acts from liability when such acts are commonly accepted, even if they have prejudicial effects.[35] Furthermore, in *Metalclad*, it was held that the motivation, and the intent, of adopting the 'Ecological Decree' need not be taken into account.[36] This leads to focus on the effect of the measures regardless of whether the disputed act was a *bona fide* measure.[37]

Some scholars argue that the host State cannot arbitrarily, through its domestic legislation, nullify any principle that is universally accepted by international law (such as banning immediate compensation in cases of indirect expropriation).[38] On the other hand, others argue that there is no rule that is 'globally-accepted' which forbids a State to regulate otherwise.[39] In their view, it is legitimate to ban immediate compensation as long as the public interest is pursued, and the legislation has a general and impersonal character.[40] Others advocate the notion of the supremacy of international law over municipal law.[41] The PCIJ held that a State cannot rely on its legislation to limit its international obligations.[42] Once a State signs an international treaty, the terms of that treaty become enforceable in the signatory State.

2.2. The Severity of the Measures

It is argued that in order to allege indirect expropriation, the measures' effects should be equivalent to direct expropriation.[43] Thus, compensation should be paid if ostensible action dramatically affected the foreign investor.[44] Deciding

---

[33] The same conclusion was reached in *Tecnicas Medioambientales Tecmed SA v Mexico* (2003) Case No. ARB (AF)/00/2. The tribunal asserted that the government's intentions were less significant than the impact of the measures on the investors. Peter Leon, 'Creeping Expropriation of Mining Investments: an African Perspective' (2009) 27(4), *Journal of Energy & Natural Resources Law*, 606.

[34] Rudolf Dolzer & Christoph Schreuer cited Reisman & Sloane, *op. cit.,* 104.

[35] Bjorn Kunoy, *op. cit.*, 470.

[36] Ibid., 471.

[37] Ibid.

[38] Surya Subedi cited Hull in Malcolm Evans, *op. cit.,* 732.

[39] Ibid., 732.

[40] Ibid., 732.

[41] Stephen Schwebel. *op. cit.,* 387-388.

[42] Ibid., 388.

[43] Bjorn Kunoy, *op. cit.,* 473.

[44] Ian Brownlie, *op. cit.,* 518, Georg Schwarzenberger, *op. cit.,* 118.

how to determine the deprivation of the utility of the investment is controversial. Some scholars argue that, in order to consider a breach as acute, the investor should suffer financial harm.[45] Others assert that the detriment should extend beyond economic loss[46] to include intangible interest, such as reputation and inconvenience.[47] Many tribunals base their decisions on the economic impact on the investor.[48]

In the *Goetz v Burundi* case, the ICSID tribunal held that the revocation of a free-zone status halted all of the investor's activities,[49] and the impact of this measure was similar to expropriation.[50] Moreover, a North American Free Trade Agreement (NAFTA) tribunal held that the refusal of the local authority to grant a construction permit to the investor was considered as indirect taking.[51] Additionally, in the *Cement Shipping v Egypt* case, the ICSID tribunal decided that the prohibition of importing cement in the territory of Egypt, which was essential to the investor's cement distribution business,[52] constituted indirect taking, on the ground that such a measure paralysed the investor's activities.[53] In *Tecmed v Mexico,* the tribunal also found that the refusal to renew a permit allowing the use of landfill caused substantial deprivation of the value of the investment.[54] However, in *LG&E*, the tribunal found that the mere diminution of profits could not be equivalent to indirect expropriation.[55]

Furthermore, some tribunals held that the most significant part of the measure is the effect,[56] namely it is immaterial to take into account the motive

---

[45] Ulrich Schroeter, 'General Provisions: Article 25' in Ingeborg Schwenzer, *Commentary on the UN Convention on the International Sale of Goods* (Oxford University Press, 2014), 409.
[46] Roy Goode, Herbert Kronke, and Ewan Mckendrick, *Transnational Commercial Law* (Oxford University Press, 2011), 297.
[47] Michael Bridge, 'Avoidance for Fundamental Breach of Contract under the UN Convention on the International Sale of Goods' (2010) 59(4), *International and Comparative Law Quarterly*, 918.
[48] Rudolf Dolzer & Christoph Schreuer, *op. cit.,* 99-129.
[49] August Reinisch, 'Introductory Note to International Centre for Settlement of Investment Disputes (ICSID): *LG&E Energy Crop., LG&E Capital Crop., LG&E International INC. v the Argentine Republic* (2007) 46(1) *International Legal Materials*, 38.
[50] Rudolf Dolzer & Christoph Schreuer, *op. cit.,* 107.
[51] Art 1110 NAFTA, *Metalclad v Mexico case*, Case No. ARB(AF)/97/1, Rudolf Dolzer & Christoph Schreuer, *op. cit.,* 107-108.
[52] Peter Leon, *op. cit.,* 605.
[53] *Middle East Cement Shipping and Handling Co. S.A. v Arab Republic of Egypt* (2002), Case No. ARB/99/6.
[54] *Tecmed v Mexico case*, Case No. ARB (AF)/00/2. Anna Luca in Giorgio Sacerdoti, *op. cit.,* 64, Bjorn Kunoy, *op. cit.,* 472.
[55] Charles Brower & Stephan Schill, *op. cit.,* 486, Zeyad Alqurashi, 'Indirect Expropriation in the Field of Petroleum' (2004) 5(6) *The Journal of World Investment & Trade*, 911.
[56] *Compania de Aguas del Aconquija SA and Vivendi Universal SA v Argentine Republic case*, Case No. ARB/97/3, Alan Redfern & Martin Hunter, *op. cit.,* 500.

of the host State's measures which amount to indirect expropriation, such as environmental reasons[57] or political reorientation,[58] as long as the effect deprives the investor of the expected benefit of the asset.[59] Environmentalists argue that it is unrealistic to depend on the 'sole effect doctrine' and neglect the regulatory situation of a State.[60] According to this doctrine, there is no room for regulating environmental matters without compensating every effected investor.[61]

In the case of *Pope & Talbot*, the investor was obliged to pay export fees on manufactured wooden boards which exceeded 14.7 billion board feet, whereas smaller quantities were free. The investor claimed deprivation of economic interests. The claim was based on the reduction in quantity of exports in order to pass the boundaries without fees. The tribunal held that the deprivation was not substantial enough to amount to indirect expropriation.[62] In this respect, in *Siemens AG v Argentine Republic*, the tribunal noted that each State's isolated measure might not amount to indirect expropriation, but the cumulative effect of several 'creeping' measures might deprive the investor of the use, value and enjoyment of the investment.[63]

2.3.Regulatory Power

A State has the power to regulate in certain circumstances. This power is regarded as an exception for not compensating the affected investor even if the action taken could be interpreted as an indirect expropriation. There are a number of conditions governing this exemption.[64]

First, the State should not breach any contractual obligations that it has towards a foreign investor. Second, the State can create regulatory statutes merely when such statutes are non-discriminatory, i.e. they apply both to domestic and foreign investors. Finally, the measure should appeal to the

---

[57] *Compania del Desarrollo de Santa Elena SA v Republic of Costa Rica case*, Case No. ARB/ 96/1.
[58] *Phillips Petroleum Co. Iran v The Islamic Republic of Iran case.* 21 IRAN-U.S. C.T.R.
[59] Alan Redfern & Martin Hunter, *op. cit.,* 500.
[60] Rudolf Dolzer, 'Indirect Expropriation: New Developments?' (2003) 11 *New York University Environmental Law Journal*, 92.
[61] Ibid., 92.
[62] Rachel Edsall, 'Indirect Expropriation under NAFTA and DRCAFTA: Potential Inconsistencies in the Treatment of State Public Welfare Regulations' (2006) 86, *Boston University Law Review*, 942-943.
[63] *Siemens AG v Argentine Republic*, Case No. ARB/02/8. Alan Redfern & Martin Hunter *op .cit.,* 501, *Enron Creditors Recovery Corporation and Ponderosa Assets, L.P. v Argentine Republic,* [2007] Case No. ARB/01/3.
[64] Charles Brower & Stephan Schill, *op. cit.,* 484.

general welfare.[65] This was held in *Methanex Corporation v United States of America* when the State banned a harmful gasoline additive containing methanol while the investor was a producer of this substance.[66] The US Model BITs articulate that legitimate public objectives do not constitute indirect taking.[67]

Many investment treaties, such as the North American Free Trade Agreement[68] (NAFTA),[69] provide significant protection to the foreign investor. In particular, NAFTA prohibits direct and indirect expropriation except for a public purpose.[70] Regulations for public purpose should be implemented in a non-discriminatory manner and in accordance with due process of law. Moreover, the State should compensate the foreign investor adequately, promptly and effectively.[71] For example, a new legislation outlaws all gambling halls, which mostly belong to foreign investors, to preserve public morals,[72] or a new decree bans billboard advertising on highways to reduce accidents. This dramatically affects the inventor.[73] In these cases, if the State respects the international minimum standard of fair and equitable treatment, it will not generally be accused of indirect expropriation.[74] However, in *Compania del Desarrollo de Santa Elena SA v Republic of Costa Rica*, the ICSID tribunal affirmed that the State should compensate the investor for deprivation of the interest, although the purpose of the indirect expropriation was legitimate and classified as a public purpose.[75] Moreover, some commentators suggest that even if the State duly uses the right to regulate, the investor should be compensated for the results of the action when such results

[65] Alan Redfern & Martin Hunter, *op. cit.,* 501.
[66] *Methanex Corporation v United States of America.* Case No. 44 ILM 1345 [2005], Ibid., 501, Gary Born, *op. cit.,* 434.
[67] Rudolf Dolzer & Christoph Schreuer, *op. cit.,* 102-103.
[68] Between Canada, Mexico and the United States.
[69] Also US-Argentina BIT Article 3(1), Energy Charter Treaty & Jordan – USA BIT. Surya Subedi in Malcolm Evans, *op. cit.*, 744, Gary Born, *op. cit.*, 412-430, Alan Redfern & Martin Hunter, *op. cit.,* 496.
[70] Surya Subedi in Malcolm Evans, *op. cit.*, 740.
[71] Bronwyn Pavey & Tim Williams, 'The North American Free Trade Agreement: Chapter11' (26 February 2003) <http://publications.gc.ca/Collection-R/LoPBdP/inbrief/prb0254-e.htm> accessed 13 May 2015, Joy Cherian, *Investment Contracts and Arbitration: The World Bank Convention on the Settlement of Investment Disputes*, (Leyden: A. W. Sijthoff, 1975), 88-89.
[72] Andrew Newcombe, 'The Boundaries of Regulatory Expropriation in International Law' (2005) 20(1), *Foreign Investment Law Journal*, 3-4.
[73] Ibid., 3-4.
[74] Ibid., 40. This conclusion was reached in: *Parkerings-Compagniet v Republic of Lithuania.* The tribunal noted that a State is prohibited to act unfairly or inequitably towards foreign investors in the exercise of its legitimate power. Alan Redfern & Martin Hunter, *op. cit.,* 492.
[75] *Compania del Desarrollo de Santa Elena SA v Republic of Costa Rica.* Case No. ARB/96/1.

significantly impair the investor's property.[76] Nevertheless, changing economic, political or social circumstances compel the State to change its legal status.[77] The use of regulatory power is likely to be significantly limited if a large volume of adversely affected investors seek compensation.[78] Furthermore, some scholars assert that the legal stability requirement does not require a State's legal system to remain frozen in the time of the investment[79] and not all States' measures affecting foreign property can be termed as an indirect expropriation,[80] such as subjecting the foreign assets to taxation[81] or trade restrictions regarding licenses or quotas.[82] Others argue that, under the principles of justice and equity, no State is allowed, whatever the purpose is, to enact legislation or issue measures that are equivalent to indirect expropriations without an appropriate compensation.[83] In the *Iran-US* case, the tribunal affirmed that even if the regulations are lawful, the aggrieved investor should be compensated.[84] The UN Declaration on Permanent Sovereignty over Natural Resources[85] emphasises that a State should exercise its sovereignty over its natural resources.[86] This concept reinforces the legitimacy of regulating measures for a public purpose.

2.4.Measures' Duration

In the case of *LG&E International Inc v Argentina,* the tribunal considered the duration of the State's measures to decide whether they amount to indirect expropriation.[87] In *S.D Myers v Canada*, the investor was a firm engaged in producing PCBs (Polychlorinated Biphenyls) in Canada and exporting them to the US. However, Canada imposed an export ban. The tribunal refused to regard such a measure as indirect expropriation due to the temporary nature of

---

[76] Zeyad Alqurashi, *op. cit.,* 915.
[77] Ibid., 910.
[78] Rudolf Dolzer & Christoph Schreuer, *op. cit.,*120, Charles Brower & Stephan Schill, *op. cit.,* 483.
[79] Alan Redfern & Martin Hunter, *op. cit.,* 491.
[80] Ian Brownlie, *op. cit.,* 509.
[81] Krista Schefer, *op. cit.,* 207.
[82] Ian Brownlie. *op. cit.,* 509.
[83] Surya Subedi cited Hull in Malcolm Evans, *op. cit.,* 732.
[84] Veijo Heiskanen, 'The Doctrine of Indirect Expropriation in Light of the Practice of the Iran-United States Claims Tribunal' (2007) 8(2) *The Journal of World Investment & Trade*, 218-227.
[85] Permanent Sovereignty over Natural Resources, General Assembly Resolution, 1803 (XVII), New York (14 December 1962).
[86] Ian Brownlie, *op. cit.*, 516-517.
[87] Alan Redfern & Martin Hunter, *op. cit.*, 498.

the measure.[88] Furthermore, in the case of *Suez v Argentina,* the tribunal refused to consider the refusal to adjust the tariffs as an indirect taking on the ground that the effect should amount to 'a substantial, permanent deprivation' of the investment.[89] Moreover, in the *Telenor v Hungary* case, the tribunal found that the effects of imposing a levy were not indirect expropriation on the ground that it was not a permanent action.[90] However, if the investor's main activity is producing seasonal goods, and the State has adopted impermanent measures, this will hinder the production process, as producing such goods at the end of their season will impair their value.[91] Remarkably, it is argued that financial subsidiaries given by host States to bodies which practice the same activity as the foreign investor may have adverse effects on the foreign investor and may be considered as indirect taking.[92] On the contrary, the PCIJ considered such subsidiaries as transient circumstances, which are subject to change.[93]

2.5.Investor's Control

By this criterion, the affected investor loses the ability to control the project and make decisions due to the State's restrictive measures. Therefore, deprivation of the economic benefit of an investment does not necessarily mean that expropriation has occurred as long as the investor maintains control over his investment.[94] However, the sole control over the entity of the investment, following the destruction of the economic purpose of the investment through a new legislation, may be worth nothing.[95]

An ICSID tribunal held that although Argentina violated the contract by its measures, which caused less profit, there was no indirect expropriation as long as the investor remained in control of the investment.[96] Further, in *Tippetts,* the tribunal rejected the allegation by the claimant, who owned 50% in a joint venture with an Iranian company, that the appointment of a new manager by the Iranian government constituted an indirect expropriation.[97] This measure

---

[88] Zeyad Alqurashi, *op. cit.*, 909-910.
[89] Rudolf Dolzer & Christoph Schreuer, *op. cit.*, 110-111.
[90] Ibid., 113.
[91] Ulrich Schroeter in Ingeborg Schwenzer, *op. cit.,* 179.
[92] Peter Bossche & Werner Zdouc, *op. cit.,* 38-39.
[93] *The Oscar Chinn, United Kingdom v Belgium, Judgment*, PCIJ Series A/B No 63. Rudolf Dolzer & Christoph Schreuer, *op. cit.,* 104-105.
[94] Rudolf Dolzer & Christoph Schreuer, *op. cit.,* 117.
[95] Ibid., 118.
[96] *LG&E Energy Crop and others v Argentina Republic case*, Case No. ARB/02.
[97] Zeyad Alqurashi, *op. cit.,* 907.

did not affect the claimant's ability to participate in the management and to control the enterprise.[98] Conversely, in *Payne*, the tribunal held that such measures effectively reduced the investor's control.[99]

2.6.Proportionality Test

In order to determine the lawfulness of a measure, some tribunals compare the impact of such regulations on the investor with the advantages of public policy.[100] In *S.D. Myers v Canada,*[101] the tribunal balanced the purpose and effects of the measure and investigated whether there was a capacity to adopt an alternative measure[102] with lesser effect on the investment. This test was adopted in order to determine whether the measure fell within the State's regulatory power.[103]

In *Tecmed v Mexico*[104] the government was under pressure from the local community to oppose the investor's operation and location, which caused hazardous waste disposal in an urban area of Mexico. The national authority responded to such opposition and refused to renew the investor's permit to use the facility in order to protect the environment and public health. The tribunal made a comparison between the significance of achieving the State's goals and the significance of preventing the harmful effects on the investor. It found that responding to the community's concerns was not regarded as a legitimate purpose and such a pressure on the government did not cause an urgent situation. According to the suitability and reasonability test, the government could design measures that did not excessively affect the investor's interests. The tribunal found that the harmful effects outweighed the State's targets. Consequently, it amounted to indirect expropriation.[105] The European Court of Human Rights, for example, held that 'the State's responsibility in environmental cases may form a failure to regulate private industry.'[106] On the

---

[98] Ibid., 907.
[99] Hassan Sedigh, 'What Level of Host State Interference Amounts to a Taking under Contemporary International Law?' (2001) 2(4) *The Journal of World Investment & Trade*, 649-650.
[100] Krista Schefer, *op. cit.,* 210 & Caroline Henckels, 'Indirect Expropriation and the Right to Regulate: Revising Propotionality Analysis and the Standard of Review in Investor-State Arbitration' (2012) 15(1) *Journal of International Economic Law*, 228.
[101] *Feldman V Mexico case*, Case No. ARB(AF)/99/1.
[102] Anna Luca in Giorgio Sacerdoti, *op. cit.,* 58-74.
[103] Caroline Henckels, *op. cit.,* 230.
[104] Ibid., 230-233.
[105] Ibid.
[106] Antenor Wolf, 'Human Rights and the Regulation of Privatized Essential Services' (2013) 60(2) *Netherlands International Law Review*, 174-175.

other hand, some commentators argue that pressure on the government from community may arise from the people affected by an investor's acts. However, this may merely constitute an urgent situation.[107] Thus, there is no requirement for permanent measures against the investor.

2.7.Investor's Expectations

Legitimate expectations do not only include the State's contractual obligations being fulfilled, but also the status of the State's legal framework not dramatically changing at the time of the investment.[108] The definition of 'substantial deprivation of reaching prospective aims'[109] is not found in investment contracts, leaving the arbitrator without a benchmark.[110] In the case of *Occidental Exploration & Production Company v Ecuador,* the tribunal concluded that the stability of a legal framework is a fundamental element of fair and equitable treatment, especially if the BIT requires such stability.[111] In the case of *LG&E International Inc v Argentina,* the tribunal[112] noted that the investor's expectations should be based on the conditions offered by the State and when such expectations are violated, the investor should be compensated for damages.[113]

Some legal changes that happen within the boundaries of a normal reform of a State should ideally be predicted by any prudent investor. Thus, such transformations do not violate the investor's expectations.[114] Changing circumstances, as well as the adoption of new legislation, which may reduce the profitability of the investment project, reflect the risk which is entailed in an investment.[115] In the case *Saluka Investment v Czech,* the tribunal held that the State's right to regulate cannot be frozen and that the investor should not expect that the circumstances at the time of investment remain unchanged.[116]

---

[107] Ibid., 178.
[108] Rudolf Dolzer & Christoph Schreuer, *op. cit.,* 115.
[109] Roy Goode, *et a.l*, *op. cit.,* 297.
[110] Eduardo Grebler, 'Fundamental Breach of Contract under the CISG: A Controversial Rule' (2007) 101 *American Society of International Law*, 413.
[111] Michele Potesta, 'Legitimate Expectations in Investment Treaty Law: Understanding the Roots and the Limits of a Controversial Concept' (2013) 28(1) *ICSID Review*, 111.
[112] Alan Redfern & Martin Hunter, *op. cit.,* 290.
[113] Ibid., 491.
[114] Rudolf Dolzer & Christoph Schreuer, *op. cit.,* 115.
[115] Michele Potesta, *op. cit.,* 90.
[116] Ibid., 112.

The concept of inventor's expectations received much criticism for its bias towards investment.[117] Reliance on the affected investor's expectations could be an easy way to demonstrate that the measures constitute indirect taking.[118] The unconditional protection of legitimate expectation could fetter the State's right to regulate.[119] An objective criterion should be added to investment treaties to specify the investors' expectation, namely, what a reasonable investor of the same kind in the same circumstances is entitled to expect.[120] Some scholars relate the expectations of the aggrieved investor to the original purpose of his investment,[121] which can be determined by recognising the nature of the investor's activities—whether he is an undertaker, producer or supplier.[122]

2.8. The Situation of the State

According to this yardstick, the State's actions are carried out pursuant to goals associated with necessity, security, and minimising investments' disadvantages in the society.

2.8.1. The Defence of Necessity

A State might confront extraordinary circumstances that make the implementation of the contractual commitments difficult to fulfill (such as economic crises or wars).[123] Some scholars assert that exercising police power in wartime is lawful even if the associated measures are regarded as indirect expropriation.[124] The US Restatement of Foreign Relations Law recognises that a State is not liable for any economic disadvantages resulting from non-discriminatory, *bona fide* regulations for a public purpose under the police power of a State (such as forfeiture for crime).[125] Under such circumstances a State is not responsible for compensating affected foreign investors.[126]

---

[117] Anna Luca in Giorgio Sacerdoti, *op. cit.,* 64.
[118] Michael Bridge, *op. cit.,* 912.
[119] Michele Potesta, *op. cit.,* 88.
[120] Ulrich Schroeter in Ingeborg Schwenzer, *op. cit.,* 179, Alan Redfern & Martin Hunter, *op. cit.,* 290.
[121] Roy Goode, *et al.*, citing Mullis, *op. cit.,* 300.
[122] *Packaging machine case* [2009] Case No. 4A_68/2009.
[123] Giorgio Sacerdoti, *op. cit.,* 8-9.
[124] Ian Brownlie, *op. cit.,* 514.
[125] Susan Karamanian, 'The Place of Human Rights in Investor-State Arbitration' (2013) 17(2) *Lewis & Clark Law Review*, 434.
[126] Ibid., 434.

The US Model BITs permit the adoption of 'non-precluded measures' in the case of emergency.[127] The International Law Commission (ILC) issued strict conditions under which this measure could be used. Firstly, the country faces 'grave and imminent peril'. Secondly, the State's adopted measures are the only route to safeguard public interests. Thirdly, the State has not contributed to the necessity situation,[128] for example by declaring a war with other countries. Such conditions prevent, to a large extent, any prejudicial application of measures which may amount to indirect expropriation. In the case of *CMS v Argentina,* the tribunal held that indirect expropriation had not occurred when Argentina adopted measures freezing agreed tariffs, de-dollarising the economy and restricting public debt[129] during a financial crisis, even though such measures had a great impact on the investor.[130]

2.8.2. The State's National Security

National security may be threatened if strategic assets, such as aerospace, nuclear sector, weapon production, transportation and communication, are under the control of a foreign investor.[131] The investor may misuse the access to secret information or influence companies to adopt strategies that benefit the investor's home State.[132] In such a case, the State may adopt measures to safeguard its national security, such as withdrawal or denial of certain authorisations that may adversely affect the investor. Such measures are unlikely to be regarded as an indirect expropriation. This is especially the case if the investor violates the 'Santiago Principles'.[133] These Principles[134] impose obligations on the investor, such as the prohibition of misusing investor's influence, in order to protect local security.[135] Measures in significant industries, such as inland shipping, are often excluded from the protection of the BIT.[136] Consequently, the State can freely regulate the affairs of this sector.

---

[127] Giorgio Sacerdoti, *op. cit.,* 11.
[128] Ibid., 11.
[129] Ibid., 4, 11.
[130] Rudolf Dolzer & Christoph Schreuer, *op. cit.,* 113.
[131] Michele Barbieri, 'Sovereign Wealth Funds as Protected Investors under BITs and the Safeguard of the National Security of Host States' in Giorgio Sacerdoti, *op. cit.,* 131-133.
[132] Ibid., 131-133.
[133] Ibid., 136-149.
[134] These Principles are not binding, but when adopted by investment treaties, their nature converts to binding principles. Sovereign Wealth Funds: Generally Accepted Principles and Practices 2008 ('Santiago Principles').
[135] Michele Barbieri in Giorgio Sacerdoti, *op. cit.,* 149-151.
[136] Gary Born, *op. cit.,* 434.

2.8.3.Impact of Investment

An investment may severely affect the local life of a State contrary to what was foreseen. For example, investments may cause severe impact on environmental degradation, the livelihood of the nationals, cultural identity, political stability and public morals.[137] Such consequences increase the likelihood of governmental regulations, which may distinctly disadvantage the investor. Thus, a State may regulate against some investment activities, such as depriving a community of its holy properties.[138] These activities would not be protected, even if such regulations amount to indirect expropriation.[139] If, for example, an investor uses cheap colours to manufacture clothes, and these clothes cause skin cancer, consumer protection associations may object to such action and invoke the interference of the government to preserve consumer safety.

Some claim that suitable governmental legislation cannot be achieved if every single negatively affected investor seeks recompense.[140] An ICSID tribunal observed that privatising essential services, such as electricity, gas and water utilities, to foreign investment companies may affect millions of people.[141] Thus, it is vital to endorse regulatory reforms to guarantee that foreign investment privatisation works properly and to ensure that it is sufficient and reasonably priced. Furthermore, States should adopt the necessary measures to protect affected people from the negative outcomes of investments.[142]

2.9.Contractual Obligations and the Host State's Promises

The violation of contractual obligations is a valid criterion to assess the extent of the illegality of indirect expropriation.[143] If the arbitrator belongs to a country governed by civil law, which glorifies the contract as a source of obligation, it is likely that priority will be given to contractual obligations even if the measures are adopted for a public purpose.[144] In the case of *Biwater Gauff v Tanzania*, the investor claimed that the annulment of the contract

[137] Peter Bossche & Werner Zdouc, *op. cit.,* 14, 17.
[138] Susan Karamanian, *op. cit.,* 435.
[139] Ibid., 435.
[140] Peter Leon, *op. cit.,* 610.
[141] Antenor Wolf, *op. cit.,* 170.
[142] Ibid., 171-174.
[143] This was held in the case *Continental Casualty v Argentina*. Michele Potesta, *op. cit.,* 101, Surya Subedi in Malcolm Evans, *op. cit.,* 749.
[144] Eduardo Grebler, *op. cit.,* 411, Rudolf Dolzer & Christoph Schreuer, *op. cit.,* 122.

without cause violated the contractual obligations and amounted to indirect expropriation.[145] The tribunal rejected the claim and regarded the formal termination of the contract as an ordinary contractual characteristic, which could not amount to indirect expropriation.[146]

In *Siemens AG v Argentina,* the ICISD tribunal held that the measure was indirectly expropriative as the State used its regulatory power over the investor instead of acting as a contracting party. The contract was invalidated by a unilateral decision through precedential decree.[147] In order to be safe, an 'umbrella clause' needs to be included in the contract. This means that all contractual obligations between the State and home State of the investor will be protected under the BIT. This puts pressure on the host State to respect the protection terms of the contract.[148]

Furthermore, a new regulation which breaches a State's promises[149] constitutes indirect expropriation in most circumstances.[150] In many cases, the State offers assurances against any legal changes which would be unfavourable to the investor's interests in order to reinforce the investment. These assurances create acquired rights for investors. A failure by the State to respect such assurances may amount to indirect expropriation because it deprives the investor of the investment's benefits.[151] This conclusion was reached in the case of *CME v Czech Republic*.[152] Some scholars assert that the claim of indirect expropriation does not immunise investors from regulatory alteration unless the State promised to refrain from such modification.[153]

In the case of *Revere Copper v OPIC*, the parties concluded an agreement which did not impose any further taxes on the investor.[154] However, the newly elected government announced that an increase in the revenues had to be paid by the investor. The tribunal found that such a measure impeded the investor from effectively controlling the enterprise. As a result, the government decision was repudiated.[155] Furthermore, in the case of *Metalclad v US*

---

[145] Bjorn Kunoy, *op. cit.,* 483.
[146] Rudolf Dolzer & Christoph Schreuer, *op. cit.,* 110.
[147] *Siemens AG v Argentina case*, Case No. ARB/02/8. Peter Leon, *op. cit.,* 607-608.
[148] Margaret Moses *op. cit.,* 245.
[149] This was held in *Parkerings-Compagniet AS v Republic of Lithuania* (2007) Case No. ARB/05/8.
[150] Michele Potesta, *op. cit.,* 89.
[151] Alan Redfern & Martin Hunter, *op. cit.,* 498-500.
[152] Ibid., 499.
[153] Charles Brower & Stephan Schill, *op. cit.,* 488.
[154] *Revere Copper and Brass Incorporated v Overseas Private Investment Corporation* (1980) Case No. 628 F.2d 81.
[155] Rudolf Dolzer & Christoph Schreuer, *op. cit.,* 105-106.

Investor,[156] the investor had received guarantees from the federal authorities that he would be granted all the required licenses in the investment's life. Despite this, the local authority refused to give a building authorisation for an investment plant. The tribunal regarded this measure as an indirect expropriation.[157] Moreover, a United Nations Commission on International Trade Law (UNCITRAL) tribunal decided in favour of one investor, who claimed against the policy adopted by the Indian government, which caused excessive delay (nine years) in order to enforce an international arbitration award. The government had breached its promise to provide 'effective means' in the investment dispute resolution process.[158]

2.10.Obligations under International Conventions

A problem arises when a State is committed to an international obligation that contradicts the BIT's obligations of protecting foreign investors. For example, Indonesia is bound by such international obligations. It is a party to the Convention on Biological Diversity and Statement of Forest Principles[159] that commits States to ban any procedures that are likely to have considerable impact on the environment.[160] Indonesian Forestry Law was promulgated to protect forests. It helps regulate erosion, hydrology, and the preservation of plant and animal diversity.[161] Mining investment was affected by such law which prohibits open-cast mining in protected forests. It was difficult to claim that such a law amounted to indirect taking because the law prohibits only surface mining in specific areas, whereas underground mining is still permitted. Consequently, the effects were not serious.[162]

Additionally, the World Health Organization (WHO) Framework Convention on Tobacco Control (FCTC) obliges the parties to adopt regulatory measures in production and taxation of tobacco products.[163] The FCTC also encourages parties to adopt stricter measures in order to protect

---

[156] Bjorn Kunoy, *op. cit.,* 472.
[157] Ibid., 472.
[158] Vyoma Jha, 'International Investment Treaty Implications for the Indian Position on Nuclear Liability' (2014) 17(1) *Journal of Risk Research*, 82-83.
[159] Kyla Tienhaara, 'What You Don't Know Can Hurt You: Investor-State Disputes and the Protecting of the Environment in Developing Countries' (2014) 6(4) *Global Environmental Politics*, 87-92.
[160] Art 14 Convention on Biological Diversity Foreign. Lorenz Cotula, *op. cit.,* 73.
[161] Kyla Tienhaara, *op. cit.,* 87-92.
[162] Ibid., 87-92.
[163] WHO Framework Convention on Tobacco Control 2005.

public health.[164] A tobacco company began arbitration proceedings to challenge an Australian legislation which imposed requirements for cigarette packs on the grounds that such measures constituted indirect expropriation.[165] The Australian legislation provided that plain cigarette packs had to contain graphic health warning. The New Zealand government is waiting for the decision before issuing similar anti-smoking legislation.[166] Philip Morris also brought a claim against Uruguay for new 'cigarette-labeling measures' which required manufacturers to increase the size of illustrative health warnings from 50% to 80% on the front and back of cigarette packs. Philip Morris described the requirement as 'excessive' and that it would destroy its trademark, adding that 50% sufficed to warn consumers about the harmful effects of smoking.[167] The host State should demonstrate the stimuli to adopt such measures, such as the prevalence of tobacco in its territory, the public health crisis and the absence of alternative methods with a lesser effect on the investors, in order for such measures to not be regarded as indirect expropriation.[168]

2.11.Human Rights

One of the core principles of the UN Human Rights Council is the duty of a State to protect human rights. Foreign investors should also bear such a basic responsibility.[169] Moreover, refraining from indirect expropriation measures reflects the duty to respect human rights.[170] Many municipal laws, such as Cambodia's Investment Act 1994, restrict the government's power to expropriate investments indirectly.[171]

In 2013, a factory building collapsed and 1000 workers were killed in Bangladesh whilst working for a foreign investment.[172] A State should not neglect individuals who work under inadequate conditions. On the contrary, a State should promote and conform to the rules on minimum working

---

164 Tsai Lin, 'The Status of FCTC in the Interpretation of Compensable Indirect Expropriation and the Right to Adopt 'Stricter' Tobacco Control Measures under Bits' (2014) 9(1) *Asian Journal of WTO & International Health Law and Policy*, 125-127.
165 Lorenz Cotula, *op. cit.,* 25.
166 Ibid., 25.
167 Tsai Lin, *op. cit.,* 127-129.
168 Ibid., 139.
169 Surya Subedi in Malcolm Evans, *op. cit.,* 739-740.
170 Susan Karamanian, *op. cit.,* 433.
171 Art 9 Cambodia's Investment Act 1994. Lorenz Cotula, *op. cit.,* 22.
172 BBC News, 'Bangladesh Factory Collapse Toll Passes 1,000' (10 May 2013) <http://www.bbc.co.uk/news/world-asia-22476774> accessed 20 May 2015.

conditions of the International Labour Organisation (ILO).[173] Such measures should not be interpreted as indirect expropriation.[174] Suppose, for example, that a petroleum company concluded a contract with a State to manufacture petrochemical products. The company could subsequently be charged under a new legislation on air quality. According to the new legislation, the company is required to install antipollution devices. It could claim that it is impossible to conform to such regulations due to time and financial constraints.[175] In such a case, a tribunal is likely to favour international legal obligations in the field of ecosystems, regardless of the investor's interests. Moreover, some found that if an investment is in an uncompetitive field, the State could issue a regulation permitting national enterprises to enter such field, which may adversely harm the investor. This State action could be interpreted as promoting the rights of the State's citizens.[176]

Some forcefully argue that a State has a duty to adopt measures in order to safeguard citizens' life, health, property and safety. The States cannot justify a failure to fulfil these duties by arguing that such responsibilities can be waived on the pretext of not harming foreign investors.[177] Thus, such measures would not attract a State's liability even if they are inconsistent with BITs.[178] However, in *S.A. v Argentina*, the tribunal held that the State must respect human rights and BIT's obligations equally. Thus, the tribunal refused to outweigh the necessity of the State's measures to preserve the right to water over the investor's rights.[179] States may rely on human rights, such as the rights to health, labour and a clean environment, as a defence to their acts which contradict the investor's interests.[180]

3. CONCLUSION

The abstract language of most international investment treaties and contracts makes the distinction between indirect expropriation and the State's right to regulate imprecise and unpredictable.[181] It is advisable to include a clause in

---

[173] Lorenz Cotula. *op. cit.,* 84.
[174] Ibid., 23.
[175] Joy Cherian, *Investment Contracts and Arbitration*, (Leyden, A.W. Sijthoff, 1975), 96-99.
[176] Susan Karamanian, *op. cit.,* 428-437.
[177] Kojo Yelpaala, 'Fundamentalism in Public Health and Safety in Bilateral Investment Treaties' (2008) 3(1) *Asian Journal of WTO & International Health Law and Policy*, 493-492.
[178] Ibid., 493-492.
[179] *Suez, Sociedad General de Arguas de Barcelona, S.A. v Argentina* case. ICSID Case No. ARB/03/19.
[180] Susan Karamanian, *op. cit.,* 432.
[181] Eduardo Grebler, *op. cit.*, 413.

the investment contract that requires the investor to comply with social and environmental matters. This can assist States in adopting measures for sustainable development goals.[182]

Adding a legality requirement term into the contract will force investors to comply with the applicable law in order to be protected. This will enable governments to regulate against investments which violate their rules without being accused of indirect expropriation.[183] Treaties may not penalise States when they regulate in order to protect public welfare.[184] For instance, the US Model BITs expel from indirect expropriation 'non-discriminatory regulatory actions … that are designed and applied to protect legitimate public welfare objectives.'[185] Worrisome phenomena occur when there is an urgent need to regulate but the government is reluctant to do so on the ground that the arbitral tribunal may consider such a conduct as an indirect expropriation,[186] especially if the applicable BIT does not contain a clause permitting legislation according to the public purpose. Article 31(1) of the Vienna Convention on the Law of the Treaties provides that the treaty is to be interpreted in the light of the treaty's purpose.[187] The main purpose of the BITs is to protect foreign investments. Interpreting the BITs in the light of their purpose would result in an outcome which would favour the foreign investor. [188] Bolivia, Ecuador and Venezuela withdrew from the ICSID, arguing that investment tribunals erode State's sovereignty and incline towards foreign investors.[189] Some countries, such as the US and Canada, revised their BITs to restrict the scope of investor protection.[190]

On the other hand, it is expedient to specify in the investment contract that a foreign investor's property should not be disturbed by any action, except from those which pursue a public purpose.[191] Peru avoided affecting the investment sector by promulgating new legislation which included a provision indicating that all contracts which were concluded before the promulgation remained valid until the expiry date of such contracts.[192] So the investments' activities continued by virtue of the non-retroactive effect of the legislation.[193]

---

[182] Lorenz Cotula, *op. cit.*, 29.
[183] Ibid., 29.
[184] Susan Karamanian, *op. cit.*, 434.
[185] Ibid., 434.
[186] Zeyad Alqurashi, *op. cit.*, 912.
[187] Vienna Convention on the Law of Treaties 1969.
[188] Bjorn Kunoy, *op. cit.*, 471.
[189] Gary Born, *op. cit.*, 419.
[190] Ibid., 420.
[191] Georg Schwarzenberger, *op. cit.*, 118.
[192] Kyla Tienhaara, *op. cit.,* 92-93.
[193] Ibid., 92-93.

The analysis should be underpinned by using case law. Otherwise, it is difficult to ensure predictability in advance and this may negatively affect the investor or the host State.

Works Cited

Primary Sources

Legislation

Cambodia's Investment Act 1994
Draft Convention on International Responsibility of States for Injuries to Aliens 1961
Permanent Sovereignty over Natural Resources, General Assembly Resolution, 1803 (XVII), New York (14 December 1962)
Sovereign Wealth Funds: Generally Accepted Principles and Practices ('Santiago Principles') 2008
Vienna Convention on the Law of Treaties 1969
WHO Framework Convention on Tobacco Control 2005

Case Law

Compania de Aguas del Aconquija SA and Vivendi Universal SA v Argentine Republic. Case No. ARB/97/3
Compania del Desarrollo de Santa Elena SA v Republic of Costa Rica. Case No. ARB/96/1
Enron Creditors Recovery Corporation (formerly Enron Corporation) and Ponderosa Assets, L.P. v Argentine Republic, [2007] Case No. ARB/01/3
Feldman V Mexico. Case No. ARB(AF)/99/1
LG&E Energy Crop and others v Argentina Republic. Case No. ARB/02
Metalclad v Mexico. Case No. ARB(AF)/97/1
Methanex Corporation v United States of America, UNCITRAL
Middle East Cement Shipping and Handling Co. S.A. v Arab Republic of Egypt [2002] Case No. ARB/99/6
Oscar Chinn, United Kingdom v Belgium, Judgment, PCIJ Series A/B No 63
Packaging machine [2009] Case No. 4A_68/2009
Parkerings-Compagniet AS v Republic of Lithuania [2007] Case No. ARB/05/8

Phillips Petroleum Co. Iran v The Islamic Republic of Iran. 21 IRAN-U.S. C.T.R.

PSEG Global Inc. and Konya Ilgin Elektrik Üretim ve Ticaret Limited Sirketi v Republic of Turkey [2007] Case No. ARB/02/5

Siemens AG v Argentine Republic. Case No. ARB/02/8

Suez, Sociedad General de Arguas de Barcelona, S.A. v Argentina. ICSID Case No. ARB/03/19

Tecmed v Mexico. Case No. ARB (AF)/00/2

Secondary Sources

Books

Born G, *International Arbitration: Law and Practice*, Netherlands: Wolters Kluwer, 2012

Bossche P & Zdouc W, *The Law and Policy of the World Trade Organization,* Cambridge University Press, 2014

Brownlie I, *Principles of Public International Law*, Oxford University Press, 2003

Cherian J, *Investment Contracts and Arbitration: The World Bank Convention on the Settlement of Investment Disputes*, Leyden: A. W. Sijthoff, 1975

Cotula L, *Foreign Investment, Law and Sustainable Development: A Handbook on Agriculture and Extractive Industries*, London International Institute for Environment and Development, 2014

Dolzer R, & Schreuer, C. *Principles of International Investment Law,* Oxford University Press, 2012

Evans M, *International Law*, Oxford University Press, 2014

Goode R, Kronke H & Mckendrick E, *Transnational Commercial Law*, Oxford University Press, 2011

Moses M, *The Principles and Practice of International Commercial Arbitration,* Cambridge University Press, 2012

Redfern A, & Hunter, M. *Redfern and Hunter on International Arbitration*, Oxford University Press, 2009

Sacerdoti G, *General Interests in International Investment Law*, Cambridge University Press, 2014

Schefer K, *International Investment Law*. Cheltenham, Edward Elgar Publishing, 2013

Schwarzenberger G, *Foreign Investment and International Law*, London: Steven & Sons, 1969

Schwebel S, *Justice in International Law*, Cambridge University Press, 1994

Schwenzer I, *Commentary on the UN Convention on the International Sale of Goods*, Oxford University Press, 2014

Articles and Essays

Alqurashi Z, 'Indirect Expropriation in the Field of Petroleum', *The Journal of World Investment & Trade* 5(6), 897-926

Bridge M, 'Avoidance for Fundamental Breach of Contract under the UN Convention on the International Sale of Goods', *International and Comparative Law Quarterly* 59(4), 911-940

Brower C & Schill S, 'Is Arbitration a Threat or a Boon to the Legitimacy of International Investment Law?', *The Chicago Journal of International Law* 9(4), 471-498

Dolzer R, 'Indirect Expropriation: New Developments?', *New York University Environmental Law Journal* 11, 64 -93

Edsall R, 'Indirect Expropriation under NAFTA and DRCAFTA: Potential Inconsistencies in the Treatment of State Public Welfare Regulations', *Boston University Law Review* 86, 931-962

Grebler E, 'Fundamental Breach of Contract under the CISG: A Controversial Rule', *American Society of International Law* 101, 407-413

Heiskanen V, 'The Doctrine of Indirect Expropriation in light of the Practice of the Iran-United States Claims Tribunal', *The Journal of World Investment & Trade* 8(2), 215-231

Henckels C, 'Indirect Expropriation and the Right to Regulate: Revising Proportionality Analysis and the Standard of Review in Investor-State Arbitration,' *Journal of International Economic Law* 15(1), 223-255

Jha V, 'International Investment Treaty Implications for the Indian Position on Nuclear Liability', *Journal of Risk Research* 17(1), 81-95

Karamanian S, The Place of Human Rights in Investor-State Arbitration, *Lewis & Clark Law Review*17(2), 423-447

Kunoy B, 'Developments in Indirect Expropriation Case Law in ICSID Transnational Arbitration', *The Journal of World Investment & Trade* 6(3), 467- 491

Leon P, 'Creeping Expropriation of Mining Investments: An African Perspective', *Journal of Energy & Natural Resources Law* 27(4), 597-644

Lin T, 'The Status of FCTC in the Interpretation of Compensable Indirect Expropriation and the Right to Adopt "Stricter" Tobacco Control Measures under Bits', *Asian Journal of WTO & International Health Law and Policy* 9(1), 123-160

Newcombe A, 'The Boundaries of Regulatory Expropriation in International Law', *Foreign Investment Law Journal* 20(1), 1-50

Potesta M, 'Legitimate Expectations in Investment Treaty Law: Understanding the Roots and the Limits of a Controversial Concept', *ICSID Review* 28(1), 88-122

Reinisch A, 'Introductory Note to International Centre for Settlement of Investment Disputes (ICSID): *LG&E Energy Crop., LG&E Capital Crop., LG&E International INC. v the Argentine Republic*', *International Legal Materials* 46(1), 36-39

Sedigh H, 'What Level of Host State Interference Amounts to a Taking under Contemporary International Law?', *The Journal of World Investment & Trade* 2(4), 631-684

Tienhaara K, 'What You Don't Know Can Hurt You: Investor-State Disputes and the Protecting of the Environment in Developing Countries', *Global Environmental Politics* 6(4), 87-92

Wolf A, 'Human Rights and the Regulation of Privatized Essential Services', *Netherlands International Law Review* 60(2), 165-204

Yelpaala K, 'Fundamentalism in Public Health and Safety in Bilateral Investment Treaties', *Asian Journal of WTO & International Health Law and Policy* 3(1), 465-500

Internet Sources

BBC News. 'Bangladesh Factory Collapse Toll Passes 1,000', (10 May 2013) <http://www.bbc.co.uk/news/world-asia-22476774> accessed 20 May 2015

Pavey B & Williams T, 'The North American Free Trade Agreement: Chapter11' (26 February 2003) <http://publications.gc.ca/Collection-R/LoPBdP/inbrief/prb0254-e.htm> accessed 13 May 2015.

Should Women Be Paid to Provide Eggs for Research or Reproduction?

Mathilde Formet†

The issue of whether women should be paid to provide eggs for research or reproduction is complex. An overview of the legal framework of the UK, the US, and some European States reflects this complexity and lack of consensus. Ethical concerns are often raised, but even if money is a driving force, it does not deprive women to freely consent nor does it constitute coercion, exploitation, or commodification. Paying for the services, not for the eggs as goods, justifies the monetary reward (no matter the provider and eggs' characteristics). Accepting this payment would only enhance women's autonomy, who are able to decide regarding their own bodies. Moreover, payment for sperm provision is allowed, and so payment for egg provision would establish equality between genders. Furthermore, altruism, an important principle of egg provision, would not necessarily suffer from payment. Currently, there are no strong safeguards, including price and informed consent. Implementation of strong safeguards is essential, and would allow for sufficient supply as well as for more women to experience childbirth and to develop research.

Keywords: human eggs, payment, reproduction and research, autonomy, ethics.

---

† LLM, Medical Law & Ethics, University of Kent.

1. INTRODUCTION

The provision of human eggs[1] by women is useful for two distinct purposes: fertility treatments, and research.[2] Fertility treatments support people who cannot conceive children naturally, through the development of assisted reproduction techniques. Homosexual couples and single men, who want to have a child on their own, may also need to use provided eggs. Likewise, so will straight couples, lesbian couples, or single women—when the woman does not produce her own eggs or eggs of appropriate quality. Egg provision is a solution for women who fear the transmission of an inherited disease.[3] Besides reproduction, eggs are essential for advances in stem cell research.

The eggs retrieval procedure is the same for reproduction and research, so the risks are identical for the egg provider.[4] The woman providing the eggs is first assessed psychologically and physically, and her fully informed consent is required.[5] She must take hormone medications to stimulate the production and maturation of multiple eggs in one cycle; which are then retrieved.[6] To achieve fecundation (i.e. the creation of a unique cell by the encounter of female and male gametes), the eggs are fertilized in a Petri dish (a tool used by biologists to culture cells) in the laboratory, with the chosen sperms to create embryos.[7] The egg provider can be unrelated to the recipients, anonymous or non-anonymous, providing the eggs for altruistic or monetary motives, or even be a designated donor to help a friend or a relative.

Since these steps take a considerable amount of time and constitute a physical burden for the provider,[8] the following question could be asked: should women be paid a fee for providing their eggs? The payment of egg providers can also be a key factor to deal with the insufficiency of supply of this precious resource.[9] Indeed, altruistic donation of eggs does not satisfy the

---

[1] The term commonly used for this procedure is 'egg donation', which implies that the provision is free and altruistic, a gift, in order to minimize its commercial implications. The issue of paying egg donors is then confusing and ambiguous, so the use of the term 'egg providers' is preferable to distinguish with altruistic 'egg donors'.

[2] John Robertson, 'Compensation and Egg Donation for Research' (2006) 86 (6) Fertility and Sterility 1573.

[3] IVF Zlin, 'IVF Treatment with Donor Eggs' (IVF-ZLIN.COM) <www.ivf-zlin.com/24821-ivf-treatment-with-donor-eggs> accessed 16 February 2016.

[4] Nanette Elster, 'Egg Donation for Research and Reproduction: the Compensation Conundrum' in Michele Bratcher Goodwin (ed), Baby Markets: Money and the New Politics of Creating Families (Cambridge University Press 2010).

[5] Seamus Burns, 'For Love or Money?' (2007) 157 (7273) New Law Journal 697.

[6] Robertson.

[7] Elster.

[8] Robertson.

[9] Lisa Ikemoto, 'Eggs, Nests, and Stem Cells' in Michele Bratcher Goodwin (ed), *Baby Markets: Money and the New Politics of Creating Families* (Cambridge University Press 2010).

needs for research and reproduction.[10] If payment can ensure an adequate supply, as Anne Phillips asks: 'what's wrong with introducing a market?'[11] Regulating the human eggs market is important to protect social values, including health and human dignity; also, to avoid corruption, abuses, and the creation of a risky and harmful black market.[12] Further, the ethical concerns of paying egg providers—such as the exploitation of women, coercion and undue inducement, the commodification of eggs and the human body, the value of human life and its dignity—are important considerations that cannot be easily dismissed.[13] Now egg donation has evolved into 'an industry comparable to sperm [provision]',[14] the question of payment is highly relevant when sperm providers are paid[15]—even though it is less intrusive and risky.[16] This different approach can be seen as paternalistic and can create unfair discrimination between genders;[17] as implies that women are not as able as men to evaluate the risks and benefits of the procedure.[18]

This article argues that there should be a regulated market to allow the payment of egg providers. To do so, the first part explains why the purpose behind egg provision should not be a condition for payment. The second part offers an overview of different jurisdictions, to better understand the complexity of the issue. The rest of the article focuses on what is paid for, the impact of payment on the motive for egg provision, and the women's autonomy. Finally, the last part questions the potential commodification of the human body and its products.

2. Research and Reproduction Purposes

Payment should not be different based on the purpose of the egg provision. Undeniably, payment for reproduction, or for research, and not for both would suggest that one is more important than the other, or that it is more acceptable to commodify human eggs, in one instance and not the other.

---

[10] Robertson.
[11] Anne Phillips, 'It's My Body and I'll Do What I Like With It: Bodies as Objects and Property' (2011) 39 (6) Political Theory 724.
[12] David Resnik, 'Regulating the Market for Human Eggs' (2001) 15 Bioethics 1.
[13] Elster.
[14] Susan Crockin, 'A Legal Defense for Compensating Research Egg Donors' (2010) 6 Cell Stem Cell 99.
[15] The Ethics Committee of the American Society for Reproductive Medicine, 'Financial Compensation of Oocyte Donors' (2007) 88 (2) Fertility and Sterility 305.
[16] Emily Jackson, *Medical Law: Text, Cases and Materials* (3rd edn, OUP 2013).
[17] Michael Fuller, 'Donor or Vendor: The Commodification of Human Eggs'(2000) 57 (2) Current Surgery 151.
[18] Elster.

Consequently, it would complicate the availability of eggs in the case of an unpaid one.[19] 'Equal pay for equal work' should prevail since the process and the burdens are the same for both purposes; even more so when the compensation is justified by 'the woman's time, effort, risk, and discomfort'- which are equal for research and reproduction.[20]

However, creating a child and creating knowledge do not have the same outcomes, and the motives for the provision are not the same.[21] A young non-donor woman expresses her concerns between reproduction and research aims:

> 'I think I'd actually have to know the person that it was for. It's partly because of the procedure involved, and also because if it's for something that's going to end up as a child, as a person, then I think if it's my genetic material, it should go to someone I trust to bring it up properly. But for scientific research, I wouldn't have the same qualms about it'.[22]

According to Titmuss and Jonas, individuals have a moral obligation to contribute to the public good, and altruism should be the motive for donation to research.[23] Nevertheless, promoting the public good is rarely a motive on its own, especially considering the risks of the procedure. It is not as touching as offering a chance to an infertile woman to bring a child into the world, making financial incentive more useful for research.

Moreover, some women see the potential monetary value of medical discovery, considering research as a business. They deem altruistic donation for the economic profit of researchers as unfair, with no adequate compensation rates.[24] Since it is a well-established practice to pay participants in biomedical research,[25] the same should apply for egg provision for research.[26]

---

[19] Ibid.
[20] Robertson.
[21] Catherine Waldby, Ian Kerridge and Margaret Boulos, 'From Altruism to Monetisation: Australian Women's Ideas about Money, Ethics and Research Eggs' (2013) 94 Social Science & Medecine 34.
[22] Waldby, *et al.*
[23] Ibid.
[24] Ibid.
[25] Michelle Oberman, Leslie Wolf and Patti Zettler, 'Where Stem Cell Research Meets Abortion Politics: Limits on Buying and Selling Human Oocytes' in Michele Bratcher Goodwin (ed), *Baby Markets: Money and the New Politics of Creating Families* (Cambridge University Press 2010).
[26] Robertson.

Even if the motives for providing eggs are different for reproduction and research, payment should be equal—as the procedure and the needs are analogous.

3. Overview of the Different Jurisdictions

Due to the ethical concerns of egg provision, there is no consensus on this issue across the world. Consequently, the International Society of Stem Cell Research—an independent non-profit organisation for the worldwide stem cell research community—leaves the issue of payment to the discretion of each country.[27] In some jurisdictions egg providers are paid; whereas, in others, even the provision of eggs as such is prohibited. This section presents some examples of the discrepancy.

In the United States of America, the American Society for Reproductive Medicine, a non-governmental organization for multidisciplinary purposes in reproductive medicine, opposes the sale of human eggs; only allowing compensation for expenses.[28] Some States only allow reimbursement for time and inconvenience. However, in other States egg 'sellers' are paid considerable sums of money; and even more for their intellectual and physical traits.[29]

Within the European Union, the sale of human body parts is prohibited by the Convention for the Protection of Human Rights and Dignity of the Human Being in reference to the Application of Biology and Medicine (Oviedo Convention). An international treaty protects human dignity and ensures the good use of developments in biomedicine.[30] Following the 2004 Tissues and Cells Directive,[31] the European Commission recommended that the States adopt the principle of voluntary and unpaid donation, with a possible compensation limited to the expenses and inconveniences.[32] Due to the wide margin of appreciation allowed to the Member States, there are different legal frameworks across the European Union. For example, a fixed sum of 900€ is

---

[27] Ibid.
[28] Resnik.
[29] Jackson.
[30] The 1997 Council of Europe Convention for the Protection of Human Rights and Dignity of the Human Being with regard to the Application of Biology and Medicine.
[31] Directive 2004/23/EC of the European Parliament and of the Council of 31 March 2004 on setting standards of quality and safety for the donation, procurement, testing, processing, preservation, storage and distribution of human tissues and cells.
[32] European Commission, Report on the Regulation of Reproductive Cell Donation in the European Union (European Commission, 2006).

offered in Spain.[33] In France, egg donation is gratuitous; therefore, payment is illegal and only travel expenses are reimbursed.[34] The same approach is adopted by other States—such as the Czech Republic and Finland. Nonetheless, Austria, Italy, Germany and Norway ban egg donations for In Vitro Fecundation (IVF); i.e. an assisted reproduction technique involving the encounter of egg and sperm in a laboratory, ex-utero, followed by the implantation of the created embryo in the woman's womb.[35]

The United Kingdom regulates egg donation for reproduction and research with the Human Fertilization and Embryology Act 1990. The Act sets the legal framework for fertility treatments, research, storage of genetic products (i.e. human eggs, sperms, and embryos), and creates an independent executive body—the Human Fertilization and Embryology Authority ('HFEA') to monitor the implementation of the Act; especially to control human embryo research and to licence fertility clinics.[36] Until 2011, reasonable expenses were reimbursed for the donation, but because it was considered to be an administrative burden, egg donors now receive a fixed sum of 750GBP per cycle of donation as compensation.[37] The HFEA permits only compensation and does not allow the creation of a market, nor the payment of genetic products. It underlines the importance of safeguards, such as the information of the risks of the procedure, and the protection from coercion through free consent, in order to avoid harmful consequences for the egg providers.[38]

Furthermore, egg-sharing schemes are permitted and enabling due to the lack of National Health Service funding and the high costs of fertility treatments.[39] Egg-sharing enables a woman undergoing IVF treatment to donate some of her eggs for reproduction or research, in return for free or cheaper treatment. Such schemes involve indirect payment for egg donation, in the form of benefit-in-kind; it is generally higher than compensation for egg donation—without adding any risks.[40]

Wilkinson argues that egg sharing is morally more acceptable than paid egg provision. This is because egg-sharers will take clinical risks anyway for their own treatments, and not just for egg provision. Moreover, they are

---

[33] Stephen Wilkinson, 'Is the HFEA's Policy on Compensating Egg Donors and Egg Sharers Defensible?' (2013) 21 Medical Law Review 173.
[34] Agence de la Biomédecine, 'Ce que dit la Loi' (DONDOVOCYTES.FR, January 2016) <www.dondovocytes.fr/comment-faire/ce-que-dit-la-loi/> accessed 16 February 2016.
[35] European Commission.
[36] Jackson.
[37] Wilkinson.
[38] Burns.
[39] Jackson.
[40] Wilkinson.

motivated to donate to have their own child; whereas, egg providers may only be motivated by money. Therefore, the principle of free consent to donate is more likely to be violated with paid egg provision, than egg sharing.[41]

Even if egg-sharing widens access to IVF treatment, and facilitates medical research, it is criticized by female patients for two reasons: firstly, the possibility that only the donated eggs are fertile and not the ones kept for their own treatments; and secondly, the lack of inequity in health system due to costly treatments which force some women to trade their eggs.[42]

Each jurisdiction is free to regulate egg provision and its compensation, through prohibition, reimbursement of expenses, payment or egg-sharing—an original way to ensure the provision. This broad discrepancy around the world emphasises the sensitivity of the issue which appeals to different interpretations of social values.

4. What Should The Payment Be For?

Allowing payment for egg provision raises ethical concerns regarding what women are paid for:

> 'are they being paid for their time, their pain and suffering, their genetic material, the number of eggs they produce, their looks, their intelligence, their ethnicity?'[43]

As most countries prohibit the sale of body parts, the payment is generally for the time and inconvenience of the procedure, not for the eggs as products. Regardless of the number of eggs retrieved, the price paid is the same, suggesting that women are paid for the service they offer, and not for their 'goods'.[44]

Instead of payment for egg provision, a form of compensation for the burdensome procedure is more broadly accepted than a market-driven payment of supply and demand of eggs. It seems to be a safeguard to avoid a black market and protect social values, human dignity and the respect of the human body. This paternalistic intervention is 'a small price to pay for promoting health and safety and safeguarding the value of human life'.[45] Compensation aims to reimburse for the time, expenses, inconvenience, and

---

[41] Ibid.
[42] Waldby, *et al.*
[43] Elster.
[44] Resnik.
[45] Ibid.

loss of earnings during the procedure; in order to return the participant in 'a position of social and economic equilibrium'[46] and to appreciate the significance of their donation. The compensation is based on actual costs; independent of the number, quality or use of the eggs and the characteristics of the donor.[47] When high payments are offered for specific traits, the intent is not to compensate for the inconvenience and time of the procedure, but to buy a specific good. Sole compensation for reasonable expenses aims to avoid this slippery slope towards the commodification of human beings.[48] However, safeguards are not exclusive to compensation, they can also be taken when payment occurs in a well-regulated market.

Ethically speaking, it is preferable for the protection of human values to pay women exclusively for the services provided and not for the eggs as such. It should be done through a fair and equal price, no matter the other factors. Such consideration has the advantage of weakening some concerns against payment of egg providers.

5. The Motives for Egg Provision and the Impact of Payment

Different reasons can motivate women to provide eggs for research or reproduction, such as altruism for known or unknown recipients; and in most cases, even if money can be an incentive, 'it is not the sole or often central reason for donating'.[49]

Studies show that women are more willing to donate for reproduction than research. These women are motivated by empathy for other infertile women, the desire of helping them to build a family,[50] and sometimes their own previous experience of unsuccessful fertility treatments.[51] Organisations use these sympathetic feelings to motivate women to donate, using emotional headlines such as:

> 'We know that life isn't all about fairy tale endings but you could be the person who helps re-write their life stories by

[46] Waldby, *et al.*
[47] The Ethics Committee of the American Society for Reproductive Medicine.
[48] Resnik.
[49] Andrea Braverman, 'Exploring Ovum Donors' Motivations and Needs' (2001) 1 (4) American Journal Bioethics 16.
[50] Waldby, *et al.*
[51] Suelen Fernanda Parames, Luciana Semiao Francisco, Juliana Almada-Colucci, Helio Sato and Joji Ueno, 'What Influences Oocyte Donation when there is no Financial Compensation?' (2014) 29 (1) Reprodução & Climatério 8.

> giving the gift of life',[52] and 'donors donate their eggs as a gift of hope [...] the real compensation is the fact that you have given a potential [life]'.[53]

In regards to the discomfort of the procedure, most of the donations are for a close friend or a relative, than a stranger.[54] It is normally more acceptable to pay the provider when there is no relationship between donors and recipients; most women would not be willing to provide eggs for strangers without an economic reward.

Nevertheless, the gift relationship is seen as an important moral value that is threatened by the monetary incentive; this is because women would be more willing to sell their eggs, rather than donate them. An altruistic society—in which women give freely their eggs to help strangers or develop research—is better than one self-interest, based in which they are willing to do it only for money.[55] However, Resnik points out that the commercial value of an object does not destroy the human ability to offer it, depending on the motives.[56] Indeed, despite the existence of paid programs for blood provision, donation remains the main way of supply.[57]

Moreover, Wilkinson fairly highlights that paying egg providers does not deprive them of enjoying altruistic feelings, and being motivated by the desire to help others. A donor testifies, 'I gained from my experience, a feeling of warmth and wellbeing remains and I think it is quite simply the best thing I have ever done'.[58] Such feelings are not dependant on the existence or absence of money, but only on the act of providing eggs for a specific purpose. Payment does not necessary annihilate solidarity as a motive, which can still be the leading one, a side one, or becoming the main one after the experience. Although some egg providers might donate solely for money, they may spend it in an altruistic way; such as taking care of a sick relative, or paying for education. Consequently, the distinction in the motives between altruism and self-interest is not black and white.

According to Philipps, only relying on the altruistic donation can lead to exploitation of the donors. This is due to an inequality, created by the

---

52 National Gametes Donation Trust, 'Egg Donation and the Law' (NGDT.CO.UK) <www.ngdt.co.uk/egg-donor/donation-the-law/> accessed 16 February 2016.
53 Gift of Life, 'Frequently Asked Questions' (GIFTOVLIFE.COM) <www.giftovlife.com/egg-donors/frequently-asked-questions/> accessed 16 February 2016.
54 Jackson.
55 Phillips.
56 Resnik.
57 Fuller.
58 Wilkinson.

expectation that fertile women should undergo demanding risky procedure, for the benefits of others.[59] Seeking altruism as the only motive is an idealistic aspiration, since donors take into account the presence or absence of compensation.[60] Also, some women may donate altruistically because they are put under pressure from relatives to help them.[61]

An egg provider can be motivated by different reasons, with altruism and money probably being the principal reasons. Even if monetary incentives persuade a woman to provide eggs, it does not necessarily mean that it is the only reason. Altruism is a noble motive, but it also bears its own limitations. It is not sufficient to merely meet the supply, so it cannot be the only acceptable reason—especially when it is not threatened by monetary incentives.

6. WOMEN'S AUTONOMY AND THE INFLUENCE OF PAYMENT

An argument used by both sides in regards payment is the women's autonomy. Reason being, the reproductive autonomy of women confronts paternalism; in order to protect the alleged weakened autonomy through monetary incentives.

On the one hand, the main argument against the payment of egg providers is the supposed risks of undue inducement, and coercion caused by the attractive power of money; undermining the autonomy of women. Money is then a strong incentive; seen as a threat to the principles of autonomy, altruism, and voluntariness, 'forcing the less willing party into trade once the price point is sufficiently high'.[62] For Richards, the threat is real when the incentives are such attractive that the offer is 'unrefusable'.[63] In this sense, the Ethics Committee of the American Society for Reproductive Medicine warns that 'payment to women providing oocytes should be fair, and not so substantial that they become undue inducements that will lead donors to discount risks'.[64] Otherwise, it can prevent women to give a voluntary fully informed consent, causing them to underestimate or ignore the substantial risks of the procedure, and the public good aspects of donating.[65] This risk can be avoided if sufficient safeguards are taken, through meaningful information and the reasonable threshold of payment.

---

59 Phillips.
60 Burns.
61 The Ethics Committee of the American Society for Reproductive Medicine.
62 Waldby, *et al.*
63 Wilkinson.
64 The Ethics Committee of the American Society for Reproductive Medicine, 'Financial Incentives in Recruitment of Oocyte Donors' (2004) 82 Fertility and Sterility 240.
65 Wilkinson.

Both legal concepts are mainly used indistinctly to ban payment. Since the consequence is the same, the free will of the women is removed due to pressures (coercion), or influence (undue inducement) exerted on them.[66] Coercion, in this context, is often by economic needs, defined by some ethicists as a form of exploitation,[67] akin to slavery, more likely to occur to students, impoverished, opportunistic or unemployed women.[68] Indeed, 'biotechnology may have great potential for advancing healing, but in the context of inadequate regulation and extreme social inequality, it threatens to convert the bodies of women into instruments for use by the more privileged'.[69]

For Cattapan, the 'economic exploitation is a reality of contemporary society', and focusing only on the egg provision is 'hypocritical in a society that turns a blind eye to wholesale exploitation in other ways'.[70] Still, other practices such as low-wage labour, pornography or nude dancing can be more exploitative and degrading than egg provision, but the payment for these services is legal.[71] Exploitation is not necessarily a negative concept in itself. This is because it is based on a relationship of utility, and each party can benefit from the other; even if the exploiter gains more, playing on the economic or sociocultural vulnerability of the exploitee. In this case, the infertile woman or research benefits from the provision of the precious eggs, and the provider benefits from the money. The recipient, seeking pregnancy, may also be pleased to help another woman with her economic problems. Likewise, the paid egg provider, seeking money, may desire to help the woman to have a child.[72] Exploitation should only be condemned after doing a balance exercise between the potential harms and benefits, from the view of the exploitee.

Baylis and McLeod[73] explain that there is no equitable way to avoid undue inducement and coercion; since the boundary between compensation and monetarization is thin. Undeniably, money does not bear the same value for every woman as depends on her economic status and financial needs. One

---

66 Fuller.
67 Wilkinson.
68 Waldby, *et al.*
69 Diane Beeson and Abby Lippman, 'Egg Harvesting for Stem Cell Research: Medical Risks and Ethical Problems' (2006) 13 Reproductive Biomedicine Online 573.
70 Alana Cattapan, 'Risky Business: Surrogacy, Egg Donation, and the Politics of Exploitation' (2014) 29 (3) Canadian Journal of Law and Society 361.
71 Resnik.
72 Wilkinson.
73 Françoise Baylis and Carolyn McLeod, 'The Stem Cell Debate Continues: the Buying and Selling of Eggs' (2007) 33 (12) *Journal of Medical Ethics* 726.

amount of money for some women can be considered as a strong incentive; whereas, for others, it may be considered as mere compensation.[74] Consequently, it is hard to draw the line between free consent, without inducement and coerced consent.

On the other hand, if women want to provide their eggs, regardless of their motives, it is their free choice; denying them such a choice is a paternalistic violation of their autonomy.[75] The paternalistic argument also implies that women are unable to make autonomous choices when monetary incentives are involved. Therefore, valid consent can only be given in the absence of economic considerations, when the donation is altruistic.[76] Oberman, Wolf, and Zettler fairly point out that these kinds of policies are framed by sexist stereotypes about women who 'cannot be trusted to make sound moral judgments about their bodies; women are expected to be altruistic, particularly when it comes to issues involving their reproductive ability, left to their own devices, women are incapable of making reasoned decisions about their own lives and bodies'.[77] Women are just as able as much as men to make a choice when money is involved. If women are well informed about the procedure and willing to do it with deliberate consent, autonomy should always prevail.

The influence of money on the women's autonomy should not be a concern to opposing the payment of a voluntary service. Money is attractive and has an impact on the choices made in daily life without annihilating the human ability to deliberate. Although it may be seen as exploitative, it is not necessarily bad when it benefits the egg providers, in a way less degradative than other lawful services. Valid consent enables a safeguard to be taken, ensuring the exercise of the paramount women's autonomy.

7. THE POTENTIAL COMMODIFICATION OF THE HUMAN BODY AND ITS PRODUCTS

A major concern about the payment of egg providers is the presumed 'commercialization of the maternal reproductive body'. The woman's body and her reproductive capacity would be considered as commodities, sold for profit.[78] Financial incentives would '[condemn] a group of women to be mined, not for a valuable metal or jewel, but for an even more important

[74] Waldby, *et al.*
[75] Burns.
[76] Cattapan.
[77] Oberman, *et al.*
[78] Cattapan.

thing, living human genetic material'.[79] It would constitute a slippery slope to standardize a trade in bodily integrity with the whole body considered as a mere commodity.[80] Ikemoto apprehends a step back to gender subordination since this specific capacity was used to justify it so 'the resulting understanding of women will consist of a little more commodity and little less humanity'.[81] Women would be reduced to reproductive resource and their bodies seen as 'fertile fields to be farmed'.[82] However, feminists are divided on this topic. For those who advance these previous arguments, paid egg provision is patriarchal and exploitative; whereas, others fight for their reproductive freedom and consider the absence of payment as paternalist—which this article defends.[83]

Nevertheless, these concerns are justified when women with specific traits, such as high intelligent quotient or tallness are highly paid. It suggests that their eggs are commercial properties that follow the rules of supply and demand.[84] Elster and Fuller denounce the commodification of the eggs, fearing a slippery slope towards the commodification of embryos and babies when particular traits are sought.[85] High payments for precise characteristics indicate that some traits are socially more desirable than others, which can lead to positive eugenics.[86] Future children are seen as objects, as a product which can be bought and designed to an extent and which are genetically determined, instead of recognizing their intrinsic dignity and worth.[87] Moreover, different prices are discriminatory for those who cannot afford such amounts and for the egg providers, with no desirable traits, who would not be offered the same amount of money.[88]

Refusing to consider the body as a commodity is important as it promotes values such as the respect for human dignity and human rights. Human eggs are seen as a fundamental aspect of human life and as such they have an intrinsic dignity and moral worth.[89] Furthermore, the value of eggs is beyond a price, and cannot be compared with any other object. Eggs have the capacity to produce a human life, so putting a price on them devalues its inherent

---

[79] Burns.
[80] Oberman. *et al.*
[81] Ikemoto.
[82] Cattapan.
[83] Resnik.
[84] The Ethics Committee of the American Society for Reproductive Medicine.
[85] Elster and Fuller.
[86] The Ethics Committee of the American Society for Reproductive Medicine.
[87] Oberman, *et al.*
[88] Resnik.
[89] Ibid.

dignity. For Eyal, the 'body exceptionalism' prevents treating the body as a material resource with an economic value.[90] This point is also defended by religions which consider the body as the temple of the soul.[91] As Ikemoto highlights, banning payment for human products constitutes a barrier between the market value of things in the commerce and intrinsic value of human beings.[92] The same argument justifies the prohibition of payment for organs and tissues donations.[93] Resnik invokes three principles for prohibiting the commodification of eggs: the Harm Principle, Paternalism, and the Welfare Principle. According to him, it will avoid harms to people, it will promote the interests of the women willing to sell their eggs and it will protect social values.[94]

However, since the payment is for the service, and not for the eggs as products, it does not destroy the inherent dignity granted to eggs. Therefore, their commodification should not be a concern, subject to equal payments for egg providers regardless of their characteristics. Furthermore, some of the arguments against payment can be dismissed by their lack of coherence. Phillips denounces 'a potential hypocrisy in praising people when they give, yet condemning them when they seek payment'.[95] Indeed, property over the body is denied for monetary reward; but, is recognized when some parts are given to research or fertility treatment.[96] Relevant arguments are also underlined: people can charge for the use of their bodies for a variety of works, such as house cleaners or prostitution but do not have the same right for a reproductive work. Moreover, 'we cannot do any kind of work without dragging the body along' and obviously, the sale of services involving the body cannot be banned.[97] The body is already commodified in different practices, so allowing the payment for eggs provision only contributes to this trend.[98] A distinction is drawn between the self, the capacities and the body which hosts them so contracting for the use of the body's capacities does not devalue human dignity which lies on the self, and is distinct from the paid services. Indeed, as humans are embodied beings, they cannot be separated from their bodies. The sole fact that the provision of eggs involves the woman's body is not enough to justify the violation of the self, and its dignity

[90] Phillips.
[91] Resnik.
[92] Ikemoto.
[93] The Ethics Committee of the American Society for Reproductive Medicine.
[94] Resnik.
[95] Phillips.
[96] Ibid.
[97] Ibid.
[98] Resnik.

when the service is paid.[99] In the same line, Resnik denies that an individual and his body have the same moral status, so that the commodification of some parts of his body is also of that person. For him, the distinction is drawn between the whole human body and some of its parts, which sale do not affect its entirety and then do not violate human dignity.[100] The difference between selling some parts of the body such as human hair or blood, and providing eggs is not that significant; eggs only have half a human genome, and cannot create a new person on their own.[101]

There is no consensus regarding the ownership of human beings over their own bodies, and its deriving right to alienate their parts.[102] Resnik points out, based on John Locke theory, that if ownership is considered as a collection of rights to control the use of its object, then each individual owns his own body.[103] According to the paramount principle of autonomy and this so-called ownership, each individual is then free to make choices about his own body. Payment of egg providers would only enhance the autonomy of women who decide to provide this type of bodily services, without commodifying their body and its products.

8. Conclusion

The overview of the different jurisdictions shows that there is no consensus in the international community concerning payment of egg providers. This discrepancy of approaches testifies of the complexity of this ethical issue.

However, as this article argues, paying egg providers does not violate human dignity and the respect of the human body; on the contrary, it restores equality between genders, since payment for sperm providers is allowed for a less intrusive procedure. It also recognizes the autonomy of women who are able to take such decisions regarding their own bodies—even if money is at stake and attractive. Regulating this market could prevent underground agreements. Even if it might be a form of paternalism, at least it is fairer and less obtrusive. Such incentives, compatible with altruism, would also deal with the insufficiency of supply, allowing more women to experience childbirth and to develop research.

---

99 Phillips.
100 Resnik.
101 Fuller.
102 Oberman *et al.*
103 Resnik.

In order to limit problems with the commodification of human body and its products, as well as concerns regarding coercion, this article suggests that effective mechanisms for a good ethical practice should be promoted. Indeed, the level of payment could be standardized based on a strict threshold, and the amount could be justified based on other similar timely and inconvenient services. The provision of eggs as a service and not as the sale of goods should result in payment. The price should be fixed no matter the numbers of retrieved eggs, their quality, or the characteristics of the provider. Such framework prevents from the commodification of eggs, eugenics, and discrimination since the amount is independent of desirable traits for a specific good. Recruiters should also vigilantly ensure that women give a fully informed consent, after receiving all the meaningful information about the risks of the procedure. With strong and appropriate safeguards, exploitation of the woman's body could be reasonably limited and eventually completely disappear. This can result in a win-win situation since each party would benefit from the egg provision.

Works Cited

Primary Sources

Legislation

Directive 2004/23/EC of the European Parliament and of the Council of 31 March 2004 on setting standards of quality and safety for the donation, procurement, testing, processing, preservation, storage and distribution of human tissues and cells

Human Fertilisation and Embryology Act 1990

Human Fertilisation and Embryology Act 2008

The 1997 Council of Europe Convention for the Protection of Human Rights and Dignity of the Human Being with regard to the Application of Biology and Medicine

Secondary Sources

Books

Elster, N, 'Egg Donation for Research and Reproduction: the Compensation Conundrum' in Michele Bratcher Goodwin (ed), in *Baby Markets: Money and the New Politics of Creating Families* (Cambridge University Press, 2010)

Ikemoto, L, 'Eggs, Nests, and Stem Cells' in Michele Bratcher Goodwin (ed), in *Baby Markets: Money and the New Politics of Creating Families* (Cambridge University Press, 2010)

Jackson, E, *Medical Law: Text, Cases and Materials* (3rd edn, OUP, 2013)

Oberman M, Wolf L and Zettler P, 'Where Stem Cell Research Meets Abortion Politics: Limits on Buying and Selling Human Oocytes' in Michele Bratcher Goodwin (ed), *Baby Markets: Money and the New Politics of Creating Families* (Cambridge University Press, 2010)

Articles and Essays

Baylis F and McLeod C, 'The stem cell debate continues: the buying and selling of eggs for research', (2007) *Journal of Medical Ethics*, 33(12): 726–731

Beeson D and Lippman A, 'Egg Harvesting for Stem Cell Research: Medical Risks and Ethical Problems' (2006) 13 *Reproductive Biomedicine Online 573*

Braverman A, 'Exploring Ovum Donors' Motivations and Needs' (2001) 1 (4) *The American Journal of Bioethics* 16

Burns S, 'For Love or Money?' (2007) 157 (7273) *New Law Journal* 697

Cattapan A, 'Risky Business: Surrogacy, Egg Donation, and the Politics of Exploitation' (2014) 29 (3) *Canadian Journal of Law and Society* 361

Crockin S, 'A Legal Defense for Compensating Research Egg Donors' (2010) 6 *Cell Stem Cell* 99

Fernanda Parames S, Semiao Francisco L, Almada-Colucci J, Sato H and Ueno J, 'What Influences Oocyte Donation when there is no Financial Compensation?' (2014) 29 (1) *Reprodução & Climatério* 8

Fuller M, 'Donor or Vendor: The Commodification of Human Eggs'(2000) 57 (2) *Current Surgery* 151

Ghevaert L and Cabeza R, 'Surrogacy, Egg Donation and Assisted Reproduction: Payments and the Conflict of Law and Policy' (2013) 4 *International Family Law* 339

Phillips A, 'It's My Body and I'll Do What I Like With It: Bodies as Objects and Property' (2011) 39 (6) *Political Theory* 724

Purewal S and van der Akker O, 'British Women's Attitudes towards Oocyte Donation: Ethnic Differences and Altruism' (2006) 64 *Patient Education and Counseling* 43

Resnik D, 'Regulating the Market for Human Eggs' (2001) 15 Bioethics 1

Robertson J, 'Compensation and Egg Donation for Research' (2006) 86 (6) *Fertility and Sterility* 1573

The Ethics Committee of the American Society for Reproductive Medicine, 'Financial Incentives in Recruitment of Oocyte Donors' (2004) 82 *Fertility and Sterility* 240

The Ethics Committee of the American Society for Reproductive Medicine, 'Financial Compensation of Oocyte Donors' (2007) 88 (2) *Fertility and Sterility* 305

Waldby C, Kerridge I and Boulos M, 'From Altruism to Monetisation: Australian Women's Ideas about Money, Ethics and Research Eggs' (2013) 94 *Social Science & Medicine* 34

Wilkinson S, 'Is the HFEA's Policy on Compensating Egg Donors and Egg Sharers Defensible?' (2013) 21 *Medical Law Review* 173

Reports

European Commission, Report on the Regulation of Reproductive Cell Donation in the European Union (European Commission, 2006)

Internet Sources

Agence de la Biomédecine, 'Ce que dit la Loi' (DONDOVOCYTES.FR, January 2016) <www.dondovocytes.fr/comment-faire/ce-que-dit-la-loi/> accessed 16 February 2016

Associated Press, 'Fertility Treatment Bans in Europe Draw Criticism' (FOXNEWS.COM, 13 April 2012) <www.foxnews.com/world/2012/04/13/fertility-treatment-bans-in-europe-draw-criticism.html> accessed 16 February 2016

Eugin Clinic, 'Egg Donation' (EUGIN.CO.UK, January 2016) <www.eugin.co.uk/faq/egg-donation/> accessed 16 February 2016

Gift ov Life, 'Frequently Asked Questions' (GIFTOVLIFE.COM) <www.giftovlife.com/egg-donors/frequently-asked-questions/> accessed 16 February 2016

Human Fertilisation and Embryology Authority, 'Egg Donation and Egg Sharing' (HFEA.GOV.UK, 5 August 2014) <www.hfea.gov.uk/egg-donation-and-egg-sharing.html> accessed 16 February 2016

IVF Zlin, 'IVF Treatment with Donor Eggs' (IVF-ZLIN.COM) <www.ivf-zlin.com/24821-ivf-treatment-with-donor-eggs> accessed 16 February 2016

Louisa Schaefer, 'Germany's Egg Donation Prohibition Is Outdated, Experts Say' (DW.COM, 12 December 2007) <www.dw.com/en/germanys-egg-donation-prohibition-is-outdated-experts-say/a-2999675-1> accessed 16 February 2016

National Gametes Donation Trust, 'Egg Donation and the Law' (NGDT.CO.UK) <www.ngdt.co.uk/egg-donor/donation-the-law/> accessed 16 February 2016

Newlife, 'Egg Donation in Greece' (NEWLIFE-IVF.CO.UK) <www.newlife-ivf.co.uk/eggdonation-greece.php> accessed 16 February 2016

Trans Gender Justice: Critical Reflections on the Conceptual Limitations of English Law, Implementation of the Law, and the Relationship with Social Progress

Divya Jalan†

Whilst trans issues have been explored in political, medical, queer theory and US legal literature, the UK's legal literature remains more limited. The Gender Recognition Act 2004 (GRA) marked a shift in the debate on trans issues from academia to implementation. This article attempts to go some way in filling the legal lacuna by engaging in a socio-legal analysis of English law's ability to provide gender justice by giving full legal recognition to all trans and non-discriminatory access to rights based on this. First, drawing upon the foundations provided by feminist discourse on what constitutes 'sex', 'gender', 'male' and 'female', we can analyse the historical development of English law. Secondly, the law is historically conceptually limited by its privileging of sex over gender and its affirmation of the male/female binary as epitomised in Corbett v Corbett*. Thirdly, an analysis of the GRA and its relationship with key civil law legislations demonstrates that English law remains conceptually limited because of an incomplete shift from sex to gender and reaffirmation of the binary. Finally, a reflection upon the relationship between social progress, the law's theoretical limitations and implementation leads to the conclusion that, although the law contributes to trans gender*

† School of Law, University of Warwick (2012-2015).

justice, social change is fundamental to shaping more conceptually progressive legislation that can itself have a transformative role on society and the law's effective implementation through social compliance. Neither the law nor public policy and politics may be neglected when contemplating greater gender justice for trans individuals.

Keywords: transgender, *Corbett v Corbett*, Gender Recognition Act 2004, Equality Act 2010.

1. INTRODUCTION

Whilst trans issues have largely been explored in political, medical, queer theory and US legal literature, the UK's legal literature remains more limited. Cowan, Sharpe, Grabham, Sandland and Whittle are some of the few academics shaping academic trans legal literature. The trans community must be given greater recognition. Whilst the term 'trans' is constantly evolving, this article defines it as any person whose gender identity differs from their birth sex.[1] Gender identity is defined as one's self-identification as being a man, a woman, neither, both or somewhere else in an all-encompassing 'gender galaxy'.[2]

This article argues that the English law's ability to provide gender justice by giving full legal recognition to all trans, and non-discriminatory access to legal rights based on such recognition, is conceptually limited. Social progress is needed to overcome these limitations and promote effective implementation. In order to do so, this article firstly, situates its discussion within Western theoretical understandings of 'sex', 'gender', 'male' and 'female' as shaped by medical and feminist discourse. Secondly, it argues that English law is historically conceptually limited by its privileging of biological birth sex over socially/psychologically constructed gender and its affirmation

---

[1] Silvan Agius and Christa Tobler, Trans and Intersex People: Discrimination on the Grounds of Sex, Gender Identity and Gender Expression (2012) European Commission Report 5, 12.

[2] Dylan Vade, 'Expanding Gender and Expanding the Law: Toward a Social and Legal Conceptualization of Gender That Is More Inclusive of Transgender People' (2004) 11 *Michigan Journal of Gender and Law* 253, 261,267, 271; Home Office, 'Transgender Equality' (The National Archives) <http://webarchive.nationalarchives.gov.uk/20130128141739/http://homeoffice.gov.uk/equalities/lgbt/transgender-equality/> accessed 20 March 2015.

of the male-female binary. Thirdly, it analyses the seminal Gender Recognition Act 2004 (GRA) and its relationship with other key civil law legislations to argue that English law remains conceptually limited currently because it manifests an incomplete shift from the idea of 'biological' birth sex to social/psychological gender and reaffirms the male/female binary. Finally, it critically reflects upon the relationship between social progress, the law's theoretical limitations and implementation to conclude that although the law contributes to gender justice for trans, social change is also pivotal.

2. THEORETICAL CONTEXT

Radical feminism seeks to invalidate trans gender identities, arguing that the concept of gender is predicated on essentialist, stereotypical notions of 'male' and 'female'. [3] However, Sandland correctly maintains that feminist legal theory retains critical historical salience when discussing the emerging body of English trans jurisprudence.[4] The distinction between biological birth 'sex' and socially constructed 'gender', and the 'male/female' gender binary underpin English law. Stoller, a psychoanalyst, established the notion of sex as biological and gender as psychological to explain transsexual patients as experiencing 'gender dysphoria'.[5] Rubin, an American feminist, used the conceptual tools provided by Stoller's ideas to further define gender as the result of social norms and behaviours associated with a particular sex. [6] Feminists have used the conceptual foundations provided by Stoller and Rubin to engage in vigorous debate about the definition of 'sex', 'gender', 'male' and 'female' and their implications for gender justice. [7] The clashes between

---

[3] See: Michelle Goldberg, 'What is a Woman?: The Dispute Between Radical Feminism and Transgenderism' (*The New Yorker*, 4 August 2014) <http://www.newyorker.com/magazine/2014/08/04/woman-2> accessed 25 March 2015; Sheila Jeffreys, *Gender Hurts: A Feminist Analysis of the Politics of Transgenderism* (Routledge 2014) 3, 36- 40.
[4] Ralph Sandland, 'Feminism and the Gender Recognition Act 2004' [2005] *Feminist Legal Studies* 43, 44-45, 59. See also: Julie Greenberg, Marybeth Herald and Mark Strasser, 'Beyond the Binary: What Can Feminists Learn from Intersex Transgender Jurisprudence' [2010] *Michigan Journal of Gender & Law* 13, 16; Sheila Jeffreys, 'They Know It When They See It: The UK Gender Recognition Act 2004' [2008] *British Journal of Politics & International Relations* 328, 330-331.
[5] Toril Moi, *What is a Woman?* (OUP 2001) 21.
[6] Ibid., 23, 24.
[7] Ibid., 21-25; Jeffreys, *Gender Hurts: A Feminist Analysis of the Politics of Transgenderism*; Moya Lloyd, 'Judith Butler' in George Ritzer and Jeffrey Stepnisky (eds), *Major Social Theorists: Volume II Contemporary Social Theorists* (Blackwell Publishing 2011) 545; Sharon Cowan, '"Gender is No Substitute for Sex": A Comparative Human Rights Analysis of the Legal Regulation of Sexual Identity' [2005] *Feminist Legal Studies* 67, 70-73.

radical feminists and trans, and Butler's post-structuralist understandings of gender performativity, essentially the notion that gender shapes sex, have been foundational in shaping the trans movement.[8] The theoretical difficulties that feminist discourse on sex and gender have made apparent elsewhere underpin English law's attempt to deliver gender justice for trans by providing legal recognition and non-discriminatory access to civil rights based on this recognition.

3. The Historically Embedded Conceptual Limitations of English law

As Cowan submits, the law's ability to recognise trans identities and deliver gender justice based on this recognition will always be limited by English law's historical foundational understandings of sex, gender, male and female as exemplified in *Corbett v Corbett.*[9] These understandings have shaped both civil and criminal law.[10] This article focuses on the civil law context. As Cowan further argues, *Corbett*[11] highlights the law's privileging of the medico-legal notion of biological birth sex as the true test for determining whether one is male or female for legal purposes.[12]

Ormrod J held that April Ashley was a man because her biological birth sex was male. Her marriage was annulled on the grounds of sexual incapacity under the Matrimonial Causes Act 1973, section 11(c) because she was deemed not 'truly' capable of heterosexual vaginal intercourse with a male.[13] The fact that Ashley had been living as a woman for years and had undergone sex reassignment surgery was deemed irrelevant. As Tirohl and Bowers submit, the law was not concerned with one's 'subjective' social/ psychological perception of one's gender.[14] Ormrod J maintained that sex is

---

[8] Talia Betcher, 'Feminist Perspectives on Trans Issues' (Stanford Encyclopaedia of Philosophy, 8 January 2014) <http://plato.stanford.edu/entries/feminism-trans/> accessed 28 March 2015; Judith Butler, Gender Trouble: Feminism and the Subversion of Identity (Routledge 1990) 13; Lloyd, 'Judith Butler', 548; Goldberg.

[9] *Corbett v Corbett (otherwise Ashley) (No.1)* [1971] P 83, [1970] 2 WLR 1306 (HC); Sharon Cowan, '"That Woman is a Woman!" The Case of Bellinger v Bellinger and the Mysterious (Dis)appearance of Sex' [2004] *Feminist Legal Studies* 79, 82.

[10] See e.g.: *R v Tan (Moira)* [1983] QB 1053, [1983] 3 WLR 361 (CA).

[11] *Corbett.*

[12] Cowan, '"That Woman is a Woman!" The Case of Bellinger v Bellinger and the Mysterious (Dis)appearance of Sex', 81-83.

[13] *Corbett,* 106-107 (Ormrod J).

[14] Blu Tirohl and Imogen Ruth Bowers, 'Opposite Sex – A Discussion of Rights Under the Gender Recognition Act' [2006] *Journal of Gender Studies* 83, 84.

established by the congruence of biological factors such as chromosomes, gonads and genitalia.[15] Moreover, although the challenges to the male/female sex binary posed by the intersex were recognised *obiter*, the case highlights English law's presumption that in gender terms, one can only be male or female.[16]

Corbett's privileging of biological sex over psychologically/socially constructed gender and failure to provide explicit legal recognition to trans individuals in their preferred gender identity remained established law until *Bellinger v Bellinger*[17] and *Goodwin v United Kingdom.*[18] In *Goodwin*,[19] the European Court of Human Rights (ECtHR) unanimously held that transsexuals should have full legal recognition of their post sex-reassignment operation sex and acquired gender. The UK was held to be in violation of Articles 8 and 12 of the European Convention on Human Rights (ECHR). The court stated the essentialist, biological birth sex *Corbett* test was not appropriate anymore.[20]The ECtHR notably approved Thorpe J's dissenting judgement in *Bellinger v Bellinger*[21] in the Court of Appeal that was awaiting trial in the House of Lords at the time.

In *Bellinger v Bellinger*,[22] the claimant, who was born 'biologically' male but had undergone sex reassignment surgery, was petitioning the court to have her twenty year marriage with a 'biological' man recognized as valid under the Matrimonial Causes Act 1973, s 11 (c). The Court of Appeal applied the *Corbett* test and rejected Bellinger's argument that the scientific understanding of sex and gender identity had advanced since *Corbett v Corbett* so as to now include the immutable biological factor of brain structure and that she should fall within the intersex exception outlined in *Corbett* because not enough medical progress had been made to scientifically determine brain sex yet.[23] The leading judgement of Dame Butler-Sloss and

---

[15] *Corbett,* 106-107 (Ormrod J).

[16] *Corbett,* 102 (Ormrod J); Lisa Fishbayn, '"Not Quite One Gender or the Other": Marriage Law and the Containment of Gender Trouble in the United Kingdom' [2007] *Journal of Gender, Social Policy & the Law* 412, 420, 428.

[17] *Bellinger v Bellinger* [2003] UKHL 21, [2003] 2 AC 467.

[18] *Goodwin v United Kingdom* (2002) 35 EHRR 18.

[19] Ibid., para 71-72, 90, 101, 120.

[20] Ibid., para 82–83; Cowan, '"Gender is No Substitute for Sex": A Comparative Human Rights Analysis of the Legal Regulation of Sexual Identity',74; Alex Harris, 'Non-Binary Gender Concepts and the Evolving Legal Treatment of UK Transsexed Individuals: A Practical Consideration of the Possibilities of Butler' [2012] *Journal of International Women's Studies* 57, 59.

[21] *Goodwin,* para 53, 82, 91.

[22] *Bellinger* UKHL.

[23] *Bellinger v Bellinger* [2001] EWCA Civ 1140, [2003] 2 AC 467 para 47, 54–55, 65; Fishbayn, 429.

Robert Walker LJJ emphasizes the centrality of biological sex to English law that was reflective of wider social notions of what it meant to be male or female in the UK at the time.

Thorpe J argued in his dissenting judgement that a purely biological *Corbett* test should be revised to include psychological factors given the social and scientific progress since *Corbett*.[24] Based on this and her surgery, he recognized Mrs. Bellinger as a woman and able to consummate the marriage through heterosexual sex as required under the Matrimonial Causes Act 1973. In *Goodwin*, [25] the ECtHR concurred with Thorpe J that the UK had placed a 'disproportionate emphasis on chromosomal sex as the basis for legal identification of transsexuals given that intersex people often have gender identities that are incongruent with their chromosomal sex. [26] It also emphasized how increased social and medical progress prompted many European countries to provide legal recognition to trans in their 'new' gender identities.[27] The ECtHR recommended that the UK should provide legal recognition to transsexuals for all purposes, holding that the UK no longer had a margin of appreciation over the matter given the social progress in Europe.[28]

Goodwin, *Bellinger*, and the campaigning of trans activists led to the seminal Gender Recognition Act 2004 (GRA). [29] The GRA went further than the ECtHR's recommendations in providing legal recognition to trans identities for all purposes and gender justice.[30] Yet, regardless of the progress made by the GRA, as the above analysis of the case law shows, English law remains inherently theoretically limited. It is limited by historical understandings that privilege biological birth sex over gender, thus marginalizing trans identities by the inability to comprehend their preferred gender identification within the already limiting male/female binary. Conceptual progress in the law for trans is closely tied to wider social progress.

---

[24] *Bellinger* EWCA, para 117, 128, 132, 156–160.
[25] *Goodwin,* para 82–83.
[26] Fishbayn, 432.
[27] *Goodwin,* para 81–85], 100.
[28] Ibid., para 73, 85, 93, 120.
[29] *Goodwin*; *Bellinger* EWCA; Sandland, 'Feminism and the Gender Recognition Act 2004' 44-45. See also: Stephen Whittle, 'The Opposite of Sex is Politics – The UK Gender Recognition Act and Why it is Not Perfect, Just Like You and Me' [2006] *Journal of Gender Studies* 267; Andrew Sharpe, 'A Critique of the Gender Recognition Act 2004' [2007] *Bioethical Inquiry* 42, 42; Jeffreys, 'They Know It When They See It: The UK Gender Recognition Act 2004', 329.
[30] Andrew Sharpe, 'Gender Recognition in the UK: A Great Leap Forward' [2009] *Social & Legal Studies* 241, 242.

Moreover, as Cowan has noted, *Corbett*[31] has never been explicitly overturned in the common law. Despite the ECtHR's holding in *Goodwin*,[32] the House of Lords did not follow suit in *Bellinger*.[33] It rejected Bellinger's petition on the basis that it was bound to apply the *Corbett* biological birth sex test as the matter was an issue for Parliamentary reform and issued a declaration of incompatibility instead. Thus, as Cowan rightly maintains, using Sharpe and Sandland's phraseology, the 'spectre' of *Corbett*[34] continues to haunt English law.[35] The following analysis of the GRA will elucidate how these historical conceptual foundations continue to limit English law and inhibit full legal recognition of all trans gender identities and non-discriminatory access to legal rights based on this recognition.

4. Justice for Some and Not Others: The Theoretical Limitations of the Gender Recognition Act 2004

Prior to the GRA, transgender discrimination was only prohibited in employment and social security (broadly defined) in the UK due to developments in EU law and its effect on the common law's interpretation of the Sex Discrimination Act 1975 and Sex Discrimination (Gender Reassignment) Regulations.[36] As K.S. Radhakrishnan J recently affirmed in

---

31 *Corbett.*

32 *Goodwin.*

33 *Bellinger* UKHL.

34 *Corbett.*

35 Cowan, '"That Woman is a Woman!" The Case of Bellinger v Bellinger and the Mysterious (Dis)appearance of Sex', 81; Ralph Sandland, 'Crossing and not Crossing: Gender, Sexuality and Melancholy in the European Court of Human Rights, Christine Goodwin v United Kingdom (Application no. 28957/95), I. v. United Kingdom (Application no. 25680/94) (ECHR)', [2003] *Feminist Legal Studies* 191, 192 referring to Andrew Sharpe, 'English Transgender Law Reform and the Spectre of Corbett', [2002] *Feminist Legal Studies* 65 in Cowan, '"That Woman is a Woman!" The Case of Bellinger v Bellinger and the Mysterious (Dis)appearance of Sex', 81. See also: Cowan, '"Gender is No Substitute for Sex": A Comparative Human Rights Analysis of the Legal Regulation of Sexual Identity'.

36 Sex Discrimination Act 1975; Sex Discrimination (Gender Reassignment) 1999, SI 1999/1102; Case C-13/94 *P v S and Cornwall CC* [1996] 2 CMLR 247; *Chessington World of Adventures Ltd v Reed* [1998] ICR 97; Aileen McColgan, 'Transgender Discrimination' (Westlaw Insight, 19 February 2014) <http://login.westlaw.co.uk/maf/wluk/app/document?&srguid=i0ad82d080000014cacfe9f470d545744&docguid=I10DB0F00997211E38042969C9A35621A&hitguid=I10DB0F00997211E38042969C9A35621A&rank=2&spos=2&epos=2&td=3&crumb-action=append&context=18&resolvein=true> accessed 20 March 2015. See also: Cowan, '"Gender is No Substitute for Sex": A Comparative Human Rights Analysis of the Legal Regulation of Sexual Identity',77; Sandland, 'Feminism and the Gender Recognition Act 2004' 57-58, 60.

National Legal Services Authority v Union of India and Others, which gave certain culturally defined trans subjects access to legal rights based on their legal recognition as a third gender, the GRA represents some of the most progressive legislation on trans globally.[37]

Once a Gender Recognition Certificate is granted under the Act:

> …the person's gender becomes for *all purposes* the acquired gender (so that, if the acquired gender is the male gender, the person's sex becomes that of a man and, if it is the female gender, the person's sex becomes that of a woman).[38] [emphasis added]

A Gender Recognition Certificate (GRC) must be granted by the Gender Recognition Panel, constituting of medico-legal experts, if the applicant is 18 or above; has or has had gender dysphoria; lived in the acquired gender for two years prior to application; intends to continue to live in the acquired gender until death; or changed gender under an approved foreign jurisdiction; and complies with the requirements under section 3 which includes the provision of medical reports evidencing gender dysphoria.[39]

The GRA gives transsexuals and transgenders, those wishing to permanently transition to a male or female gender identity, legal recognition in their preferred gender identities. As Sandland, Cowan and Sharpe acknowledge, it represents a progressive shift in the law from *Corbett's* biological idea of sex to the more emancipatory social/psychological gender.[40] Sandland argues the Act reflects a progressive Butlerian approach to gender;

---

[37] *National Legal Services Authority v Union of India and Others*, Supreme Court of India, Writ Petition (Civil) No. 400 of 2012, No. 604 of 2013, 29-48 (K.S. Radhakrishnan J); Sharpe, 'Gender Recognition in the UK: A Great Leap Forward', 243-244.
[38] Gender Recognition Act 2004, s 9.
[39] Ibid., ss 1 and 2; HM Courts & Tribunals Service, 'Gender Recognition Panel Guidance' (23 December 2014)< https://www.justice.gov.uk/tribunals/gender-recognition-panel> accessed 10 March 2015; Stephen Gilmore, 'The Gender Recognition Act 2004' [2004] *Family Law* 741, 742-743; The National Archives, 'Tribunals Service: Gender Recognition Panel' (12 April 2015) < http://webarchive.nationalarchives.gov.uk/20110206182821/http://www.grp.gov.uk/aboutus.htm> accessed 12 April 2015.
[40] Agius and Tobler, 12. ; Sandland, 'Feminism and the Gender Recognition Act 2004', 47, 65, 79; Cowan, '"Gender is No Substitute for Sex": A Comparative Human Rights Analysis of the Legal Regulation of Sexual Identity', 75; Sharpe, 'A Critique of the Gender Recognition Act 2004', 37; Andrew Sharpe, 'Endless Sex: The Gender Recognition Act 2004 and the Persistence of a Legal Category' [2007] *Feminist Legal Studies* 57, 70.
See also: Cowan, '"That Woman is a Woman!" The Case of Bellinger v Bellinger and the Mysterious (Dis)appearance of Sex', 90.

the Act sees 'gender' as dynamic and 'sex' as a by-product of gender.[41] English law's orthodox construction on the basis of biological sex defining what it means to be male or female instead of one's subjective psychological/ social gender identification is destabilized by the recognition of transsexual and transgender embodiment. Nevertheless, as Sharpe submits, the GRA retains, firstly, an incomplete shift from the notion of sex to gender and, secondly, as argued by Cowan, Sandland, Fishbayn, and Harris, a male/female binary that fails to provide full legal recognition to all trans' lived gender realities.[42] The two conceptual limitations of the law are interlinked and, as Conaghan maintains, the gendered nature of the law itself and the way it genders limits gender justice.[43]

4.1.The Incomplete Shift from Sex to Gender

Firstly, as Sharpe correctly argues, although prima facie gender recognition is not dependent upon sex reassignment surgery, there is an underlying expectation in the GRA 2004 that the applicant will undergo surgery to ensure biological permanence in a preferred gender identity and social, lived permanence. [44] The Parliamentary debate over the GRA reflects how this conceptual limitation of the law is itself shaped by broader social progress. As noted by Sharpe, David Lammy, an elected representative of British society, stated in the House of Commons that 'individuals will not be able to skip from one gender to another' and 'ultimately [transsexuals] have surgical treatment if it is viable.' [45] Although Lammy's comments are not representative of all British society, it is clear that the privileging of *Corbett* biological sex and the male/female binary dominates society's ideas on recognizable gender identities and these majority views shaped the GRA's conceptual limitations.

Secondly, as Sandland observes, under the now elapsed fast-track application process for a GRC, a medical report to explain why no surgical

---

[41] Sandland, 'Feminism and the Gender Recognition Act 2004', 47, 61.
[42] Sharpe, 'Endless Sex: The Gender Recognition Act 2004 and the Persistence of a Legal Category', 60-61; Sharpe, 'A Critique of the Gender Recognition Act 2004', 39; Sandland, 'Feminism and the Gender Recognition Act 2004', 62-63, 65; Cowan, '"Gender is No Substitute for Sex": A Comparative Human Rights Analysis of the Legal Regulation of Sexual Identity', 72, 79, 91; Fishbayn, 441; Harris, 68.
[43] Joanne Conaghan, *Law and Gender* (OUP 2013) 102-103.
[44] Sharpe, 'Endless Sex: The Gender Recognition Act 2004 and the Persistence of a Legal Category', 58, 71-72; Sharpe, 'A Critique of the Gender Recognition Act 2004', 37, 39.
[45] Sharpe, 'Endless Sex: The Gender Recognition Act 2004 and the Persistence of a Legal Category', 72; HC Deb 2004, vol 45, col 19 (The Honourable David Lammy); HC Deb 2004, vol 45, col 18 (The Honourable David Lammy).

intervention had occurred was required.[46] It remains unclear what impact the refusal to undergo surgery continues to have on limiting gender recognition for trans as the Gender Recognition Panel does not publish data on how many of those given GRCs have had sex reassignment surgery. [47] Currently, s3(1) GRA requires two medical reports.[48] Under s3(3),[49] one of these reports must include any details of treatment to modify sexual characteristics undertaken or planned, emphasizing the GRA's incomplete shift from the notion of sex to gender. Sex continues to have salience as the true determinant of whether one is male or female rather than the trans individual's gender preference. This undermines the law's ability to provide recognition of trans' gender identities for all purposes and the ensuing access to legal rights in one's preferred gender identity because any recognition by the Gender Recognition Panel is influenced by *Corbett*-type privileging of medico-legal biological determinism.

Carpenter v Secretary of State for Justice[50] has recently highlighted this and the ensuing gender injustice. In this case, although the claimant was a post-operative male-to-female transsexual, she argued that s3(1) and (3)[51] were incompatible and an unjustifiable interference with ECHR, Articles 8 and 14.[52] The court failed to validate the attempt to move away from the medico-legal discourse on trans and the limiting influence of 'biological sex' in the law's ability to provide trans gender recognition. Thirwall J deferred to the legislature, holding that there was no discrimination in this case, the medical reports were necessary for the GRA's implementation and the Act was not a dishonest attempt to deviate from *Goodwin v United Kingdom*.[53] The court's inability to recognize gender injustice in this case seems at least partially due to judicial internalization of the historical socially and legally

---

[46] Sandland, 'Running to Stand Still', 256; Sharpe, 'Endless Sex: The Gender Recognition Act 2004 and the Persistence of a Legal Category', 70.

[47] Ministry of Justice 'Gender Recognition Certificate Statistics' (*The National Archives,* 24 January 2013)<http://webarchive.nationalarchives.gov.uk/20130128141739/http://www.justice.gov.uk/statistics/tribunals/gender-recognition-certificate-statistics> accessed 1 March 2014; Sharpe, 'Endless Sex: The Gender Recognition Act 2004 and the Persistence of a Legal Category', 73; Sharpe, 'A Critique of the Gender Recognition Act 2004', 39.

[48] Gender Recognition Act 2004, s 3(1).

[49] Ibid., s 3(3).

[50] *Carpenter v Secretary of State for Justice* [2015] EWHC 464, 2015 WL 849489.

[51] Gender Recognition Act 2004, ss 3(1) and (3).

[52] Convention for the Protection of Human Rights and Fundamental Freedoms (European Convention on Human Rights, as amended) (ECHR) arts 8 and 14.

[53] *Carpenter v Secretary of State for Justice* [2015] EWHC 464, 2015 WL 849489 para 14, 23–24, 27-28, 33-35 (Thirwall J); *Goodwin.*

embedded *Corbett* notion that biological sex is the true test for whether one is male or female.

Thirdly, I agree with Sharpe that the GRA's incomplete shift from the notion of sex to gender and continued privileging of biological/anatomical sex remains especially evident in voidability of marriage proceedings.[54] Sharpe notes the GRA, Schedule 4 amended the Matrimonial Causes Act 1973, s12 to make a marriage voidable if at the time of the marriage one party to the marriage did not know that the other was previously of another gender.[55] The *Corbett* idea of birth biological sex being the true determinant of whether one is male or female is emphasized within the Act thereby retaining the historical conceptual limitations within the law that have long prevented full legal recognition and protection of trans gender identities.[56]

Sandland has further criticised the GRA for failing to amend the Matrimonial Causes Act 1973;[57] trans heterosexual marriages are still voidable on the basis of non-consummation, penal-vaginal intercourse between those born with the respective genitalia, as established in *Corbett.* [58] This criticism remains salient today, although no case has raised the matter. It again emphasises the incomplete shift from biological sex to gender in the GRA thereby preventing trans recognition in their acquired gender for all legal purposes. However, it is acknowledged that the Marriages (Same Sex Couples) Act 2013 does imply a shift away from the notion of 'biological sex' by amending the law so that penal-vaginal consummation is not a ground for voidability in trans same-sex marriages.[59]

[54] Sharpe, 'Endless Sex: The Gender Recognition Act 2004 and the Persistence of a Legal Category', 73-74, 76; 79-80. Alex Sharpe, 'Transgender Marriage and the Legal Obligation to Disclose Gender History' [2012] *The Modern Law Review* 33, 41-42.
[55] Gender Recognition Act 2004, Schedule 4, paras 4 and 5; Matrimonial Causes Act 1973, s 12; Explanatory Notes to the Gender Recognition Act 2004, para 42; Sharpe, 'Endless Sex: The Gender Recognition Act 2004 and the Persistence of a Legal Category', 73-74.
[56] Andrew N. Sharpe, 'A Return to the 'Truth' of the Past' [2009] *Social & Legal Studies* 259, 262; Sharpe, 'A Critique of the Gender Recognition Act 2004', 40.
[57] Matrimonial Causes Act 1973, s 12(1)(a) and (b).
[58] Sandland, 'Running to Stand Still', 255; *Corbett.*
[59] See also: Matrimonial Causes Act 1973, s 12 (2).

4.2.The Male/Female Gender Binary

The GRA retains a distinctly male/female gender binary model that fails to provide legal recognition to trans identities not falling within this binary.[60] This is evidenced by the requirement of permanence in either of the two identities through lived reality or surgery as argued by Sandland, Sharpe and Grabham.[61] To obtain a GRC, an individual must have lived in the acquired gender throughout the period of two years and intend to continue to live in the acquired gender until death. [62] The Equality Act 2010, ss 4 and 7 protect anyone who will undergo or has undergone 'gender' reassignment from direct and indirect discrimination.[63] The Explanatory Notes define 'gender reassignment' as anyone transitioning with the contemplation of living permanently in one gender and does not require sex reassignment surgery. [64] This requirement for permanence in either the male or female gender identity forecloses options of legal recognition for the gender fluid or agender thus rendering the GRA conceptually limited in providing gender justice based on legal recognition of all trans identities.

Hines and Davidmann's sociological research emphasizes how the GRA 2004's entrenchment of a male/female binary excludes certain trans identities in the UK. This prevents trans gender justice because non-discriminatory access to legal rights based on full legal recognition of all trans identities is lacking. Hines' research on 'Christie' and 'Tasha' is particularly demonstrative. The GRA is irrelevant to Christie because she defines herself as non-gendered. [65] Tasha's birth sex is male but she has had sex reassignment surgery.[66] She is more comfortable being legally classified as female because of the practical benefits such as an earlier pension however she also

---

[60] Sharpe, 'A Critique of the Gender Recognition Act 2004', 39; Sandland, 'Feminism and the Gender Recognition Act 2004', 62-63, 65; Cowan, '"Gender is No Substitute for Sex": A Comparative Human Rights Analysis of the Legal Regulation of Sexual Identity', 72, 79, 91; Fishbayn, 441; Harris, 68.

[61] Sandland, 'Feminism and the Gender Recognition Act 2004', 50; Sharpe, 'Endless Sex: The Gender Recognition Act 2004 and the Persistence of a Legal Category', 60, 71; Sharpe, 'A Critique of the Gender Recognition Act 2004', 39-40; Emily Grabham, 'Governing Permanence: Trans Subjects, Time and the Gender Recognition Act' [2010] *Social & Legal Studies* 107, 109.
See also: Whittle, 267.

[62] Gender Recognition Act 2004, ss 1 and 2;

[63] Equality Act 2010, ss 4 and 7.

[64] Explanatory Notes to the Equality Act 2010, paras 41-43.

[65] Sally Hines, 'Recognising Diversity?: The Gender Recognition Act and Transgender Citizenship' in Sally Hines and Tam Sanger (eds), *Transgender Identities: Towards a Social Analysis of Gender Diversity* (Routledge 2010) 99-101.

[66] Ibid., 96-97.

recognizes her strong feelings of masculinity. She has changed her gender narrative to fit within the GRA's male/female binary. Indeed, as Fishbayn argues, the diagnosis of gender dysphoria needed under the GRA 2004 may also involve changing one's gender narrative to suit the medical profession's possibly heteronormative, essentialising understandings of 'male' or 'female'.[67]

Davidmann also explores the lived experiences of two self-identified non-binary trans to argue that the lack of social recognition and acceptance of these gender identities means that those who do not identify with a male-female binary are forced to strategically present themselves as one or the other for social purposes.[68] Gender injustice results; certain trans identities are not recognized by the law thus not given access to their legal rights in their preferred gender identity because of the law's limited understandings of 'sex', 'gender', 'male' and 'female'.

5. Critical Reflections on the Relationship of Social Progress with the Law's Theoretical Limitations and Implementation

For the conceptual legal framework to provide greater gender justice to all trans through legal recognition and non-discriminatory access to legal rights, a more complete shift from the notion of biological sex to gender and a move beyond the male/female binary is required. As Hines argues, gender recognition of trans identities must be uncoupled from medical discourse and practice.[69] Although this decoupling has not occurred yet in terms of the Gender Recognition Certificates, legislation such as the Equality Act 2010 and the Marriages (Same Sex Couples) Act 2013 represent conceptual progress.

Under the 2013 Act, obtaining a full Certificate is not contingent upon divorcing the spouse one married in their birth sex anymore.[70] The law has moved beyond notions of the heteronormative marriage that helped reinforce an essentialist male/female binary. The Equality Act 2010, ss 4 and 7 protect

---

67 Fishbayn, 437-440. See also: Sharon Cowan, 'Looking Back (To)wards the Body: Medicalization and the GRA' [2009] *Social & Legal Studies* 247.

68 Sara Davidmann, 'Beyond Borders: Lived Experiences of Atypically Gendered Transsexual People' in Sally Hines and Tam Sanger (eds), *Transgender Identities: Towards a Social Analysis of Gender Diversity* (Routledge 2010) 199-201.

69 Hines, 102-103.

70 Marriages (Same Sex Couples) Act 2013; Gender Recognition Act 2004 s 4 A. Previously see: Sharpe, 'A Critique of the Gender Recognition Act 2004', 38; Sharpe, 'Endless Sex: The Gender Recognition Act 2004 and the Persistence of a Legal Category'.

anyone who will undergo or has undergone 'gender' reassignment from direct and indirect discrimination in most areas of the 'public sphere' not just employment and social security as done previously.[71] Nevertheless, the Act remains theoretically limited in providing gender justice to all trans identities as it fails to even implicitly recognize them and give them non-discriminatory access to their legal rights.

The law's conceptual limitations in providing greater gender justice for trans are intrinsically linked to social progress. The historical development of the ideas of sex, gender, male and female in Western medical and feminist discourse have contributed to the conceptual limits in society as reflected by the law. The ECtHR in *Goodwin* demanded that the UK provide legal recognition to transsexuals despite the margin of appreciation doctrine because of wider social change in European states promoting such legal recognition.[72] Trans activists such as Press for Change and the Gender Identity and Research Society contributed to the enactment of the GRA 2004 and Equality Act 2010 through campaigns and political engagement.[73] Their strategic emphasis on transgenders' and transsexuals' rights and dominant social attitudes have influenced the legislature's drafting of trans gender justice legislation and the judiciary's implementation of the law.

The role of social progress in providing trans gender justice is highlighted by the decrease in legal literature on trans after the GRA 2004. The passing of the Equality Act 2010 marked a shift in focus to best practice implementation of the law and public policies designed to achieve equality for trans in employment and minimizing of hate crime, school bullying and discrimination

[71] McColgan.

[72] *Goodwin*, para 73, 81–85], 93, 100, 120.

[73] UK Parliament 'Equality Bill Committee Debates-Associated Memoranda' <http://www.publications.parliament.uk/pa/cm200809/cmpublic/cmpbequality.htm#memo> accessed 15 March 2015; Press for Change Homepage < http://www.pfc.org.uk> accessed 1 March 2015; Press for Change Homepage, 'Trans Research' <http://www.pfc.org.uk/Research.html> accessed 1 March 2015.

in sport by trans activist groups, equality bodies and the Government.[74] This shift of the debate from academia to implementation is marked by the lack of case law regarding trans under the GRA and the Equality Act 2010.

The few trans cases arising under both are regarding retroactivity, the clash between trans prisoner's rights to live in their preferred gender role to meet the GRA's requirements and security policies, and public provision of gender change medical services.[75] *Brook v Tasker* exemplifies the limits of the law in achieving practical gender justice for trans in the 'public' sphere given that its implementation depends upon social progress and public policies.[76] In this case, Miller J held, under the Equality Act 2010, that a pub supervisor had discriminated on the basis of gender reassignment against a transgender female. The pub supervisor had failed to assist the claimant when another female evicted her from the ladies' toilets and later himself prevented the claimant from using the toilets. Although arguably the law was able to deliver justice in this case and has a potentially transformative impact on society, the lack of social progress means discrimination on the basis of trans gender identities is not prevented in the many cases not brought to court.

A 2014 National Union of Students' report highlights that 50% of trans university students consider dropping out of university due to practical issues

[74] See e.g.: HM Government 'Advancing Transgender Equality: a Plan For Action' (December 2011) < https://www.gov.uk/government/uploads/system/uploads/attachment_data/file/85498/transgender-action-plan.pdf> accessed 14 March 2015; Home Office, 'Hate crime action plan: Challenge it, Report it, Stop it' (1 May 2014) <https://www.gov.uk/government/publications/hate-crime-action-plan-challenge-it-report-it-stop-it> accessed 14 March 2014; Equality and Human Rights Commission, 'Private and Public Sector Guidance' <http://www.equalityhumanrights.com/private-and-public-sector-guidance> accessed 10 March 2015; Home Office, 'Lesbian, Gay, Bisexual and Transgender people and the law' (*The National Archives)* <http://webarchive.nationalarchives.gov.uk/20130128141739/http://homeoffice.gov.uk/equalities/lgbt/lgbt-law/> accessed 1 March 2015; Press for Change Homepage, 'Hate Crime Literature' <http://www.pfc.org.uk/hatecrimerep.html> accessed 14 March 2015; Eleanor Ross 'Transgender: Is there still fear in the workplace?' *The Guardian* (London, 5 March 2015) *<http://www.theguardian.com/sustainable-business/2015/mar/05/transgender-fear-workplace-business>* accessed 10 March 2015.

[75] *MB v Secretary of State for Work and Pensions* [2014] EWCA Civ 1112, [2015] 1 All ER 920; *R (on the application of Green) v Secretary of State for Justice* [2013] EWHC 3491, [2014] ACD 63; *R. (on the application of C) v Berkshire West Primary Care Trust* [2011] EWCA Civ 247, [2011] Eq LR 499; *M v Revenue and Customs Commissioners* [2010] UKFTT 356; *Timbrell v Secretary of State for Work and Pensions* [2010] EWCA Civ 701, [2010] 3 CMLR 42.

[76] *Brook v Tasker* County Court [2014] (Halifax) (unreported).

such as lack of access to gender neutral toilet facilities.[77] Trans students feel unsafe using toilets due to their nature as a site of abuse. Although having laws explicitly recognizing certain trans identities and protecting access to legal rights on this basis goes some way in delivering gender justice, a large number of cases go unreported and it is greater social progress that is needed to prevent gender injustice in them. Social progress is fundamental to shaping more conceptually progressive legislation that can itself have a transformative role on society and the law's effective implementation in terms of social compliance.

6. CONCLUSION

This article has attempted to go some way in filling the lacuna in legal academic writing on trans issues in the UK. It has drawn upon the foundations provided by feminist discourse on what constitutes 'sex', 'gender', 'male' and 'female' to analyse the development of English law historically in terms of providing legal recognition of trans gender identities and non-discriminatory access to fundamental civil rights on the basis of this recognition. It has argued that English law is historically conceptually limited by its privileging of the notion of biological sex over social/psychological gender as epitomised in *Corbett v Corbett*[78] and English law's generally unquestioning assumption that one is either male or female. These historical conceptual limitations continue to be reproduced in English law today despite the progress made under the GRA 2004 and the Equality Act 2010. To transcend these conceptual limitations and in order for the law to have a more transformative impact in society, English law must manifest a more complete shift from the notion of sex to gender and move beyond the male/female binary to give trans individuals explicit and full legal recognition in their preferred gender identity and protection of access to their legal rights on this basis. However, greater gender justice for trans based upon the enactment of more conceptually progressive legislation and, effective social compliance with and implementation of such laws, is only possible if society progresses to become

[77]Siobhan Fenton, 'Are Universities Doing Enough to Support Transgender Students?' *The Guardian* (London, 2 February 2015) <http://www.theguardian.com/education/2015/feb/02/are-universities-doing-enough-to-support-transgender-students> accessed 14 March 2015; Abby Young-Powell and Libby Page, 'One in five LGBT students have been bullied or harassed on campus' *The Guardian* (London, 15 May 2014)<http://www.theguardian.com/education/abby-and-libby-blog/2014/may/15/one-in-five-lgbt-students-have-been-bullied-or-harassed-on-campus> accessed 13 March 2014.

[78] *Corbett*.

more cognisant and respectful of trans individuals. Neither the law nor public policy and politics may be neglected when contemplating the achievement of greater gender justice for trans.

Works Cited

Primary Sources

Legislation

United Kingdom

Matrimonial Causes Act 1973.

Sex Discrimination Act 1975.

Gender Recognition Act 2004.

Equality Act 2010.

Marriages (Same Sex Couples) Act 2013.

Sex Discrimination (Gender Reassignment) 1999, SI 1999/1102.

Convention for the Protection of Human Rights and Fundamental Freedoms (European Convention on Human Rights, as amended) (ECHR).

Explanatory Notes to the Gender Recognition Act 2004.

Explanatory Notes to the Equality Act 2010.

Case Law

Corbett v Corbett (otherwise Ashley) (No.1) [1971] P 83, [1970] 2 WLR 1306 (HC).

R v Tan (Moira) [1983] QB 1053, [1983] 3 WLR 361 (CA).

Bellinger v Bellinger [2003] UKHL 21, [2003] 2 AC 467.

Timbrell v Secretary of State for Work and Pensions [2010] EWCA Civ 701, [2010] 3 CMLR 42.

M v Revenue and Customs Commissioners [2010] UKFTT 356.

R. (on the application of C) v Berkshire West Primary Care Trust [2011] EWCA Civ 247, [2011] Eq LR 499.

R (on the application of Green) v Secretary of State for Justice [2013] EWHC 3491, [2014] ACD 63.

Brook v Tasker County Court [2014] (Halifax) (unreported).

MB v Secretary of State for Work and Pensions [2014] EWCA Civ 1112, [2015] 1 All ER 920.

Carpenter v Secretary of State for Justice [2015] EWHC 464, 2015 WL 849489.

Case C-13/94 *P v S and Cornwall CC* [1996] 2 CMLR 247.

Chessington World of Adventures Ltd v Reed [1998] ICR 97.

Goodwin v United Kingdom (2002) 35 EHRR 18.

National Legal Services Authority v Union of India and Others, Supreme Court of India, Writ Petition (Civil) No. 400 of 2012, No. 604 of 2013.

Reports

Equality and Human Rights Commission, 'Employment: Statutory Code of Practice' (2011) < http://www.equalityhumanrights.com/sites/default/files/documents/EqualityAct/employercode.pdf> accessed 20 March 2015.

HM Government, 'Working for Lesbian, Gay, Bisexual and Transgender Equality: Moving Forward' (March 2011) < https://www.gov.uk/government/uploads/system/uploads/attachment_data/file/85482/lgbt-action-plan.pdf> accessed 14 March 2015.

HM Government, 'Advancing Transgender Equality: a Plan For Action' (December 2011) <https://www.gov.uk/government/uploads/system/uploads/attachment_data/file/85498/transgender-action-plan.pdf> accessed 14 March 2015.

Agius S. and Tobler C., 'Trans and Intersex People: Discrimination on the Grounds of Sex, Gender Identity and Gender Expression' (2012) European Commission Report 5, 12.

Equality and Human Rights Commission, 'The Marriage (Same Sex Couples) Act 2013:
The Equality and Human Rights Implications for Marriage and the Law in England and Wales' (March 2014) < http://www.equalityhumanrights.com/your-rights/equal-rights/sexual-orientation/marriage-same-sex-couples-act-2013-guidance> accessed 14 March 2015.

Home Office, 'Hate crime action plan: Challenge it, Report it, Stop it' (1 May 2014) <https://www.gov.uk/government/publications/hate-crime-action-plan-challenge-it-report-it-stop-it> accessed 14 March 2015.

HC Deb 2004, vol 45, col 18 (Hansard)

HC Deb 2004, vol 45, col 19 (Hansard)

Secondary Sources

Books

Brady A. and Schirato T., *Understanding Judith Butler* (Sage 2011).

Butler J., *Gender Trouble: Feminism and the Subversion of Identity* (Routledge 1990).

Conaghan J. (ed), *Feminist Legal Studies: Critical Concepts in Law* (Vol 1: Evolution, Routledge 2009).

Conaghan J, *Law and Gender* (OUP 2013).

Davies M. and Munro V. E., *The Ashgate Research Companion to Feminist Legal Theory* (Ashgate 2013).

Enke A. (ed), *Transfeminist Perspectives: In and Beyond Transgender and Gender Studies* (Temple University Press 2012).

Hines S. and Sanger T., *Transgender Identities: Towards a Social Analysis of Gender Diversity* (Routledge 2010).

Jeffreys S., *Gender Hurts: A Feminist Analysis of the Politics of Transgenderism* (Routledge 2014).

Jones J., Grear A., Fenton R.A. and Stevenson K. (eds), *Gender, Sexualities and Law* (Routledge 2012).

Moi T., *What is a Woman?* (OUP 2001).

Ritzer G. and Stepnisky J. (eds), *Major Social Theorists: Volume II Contemporary Social Theorists* (Blackwell Publishing 2011).

Salih S. (ed) with Butler J., *The Judith Butler Reader* (Blackwell Publishing 2004).

Stryker S. and Whittle S. (eds), *The Transgender Studies Reader* (Routledge 2006).

Articles and Essays

Betcher T., 'Feminist Perspectives on Trans Issues' (Stanford Encyclopaedia of Philosophy, 8 January 2014) <http://plato.stanford.edu/entries/feminism-trans/> accessed 28 March 2015.

Bell M., 'Gender Identity and Sexual Orientation: Alternative Pathways in EU Equality Law' [2012] *American Journal of Comparative Law* 127.

Bochenek M. and Knight K., 'Establishing a Third Gender Category in Nepal: Process and Prognosis' [2012] *Emory International Law Review* 11.

Cowan S., '"That Woman is a Woman!" The Case of Bellinger v Bellinger and the Mysterious (Dis)appearance of Sex' [2004] *Feminist Legal Studies* 79.

Cowan S., '"Gender is No Substitute for Sex": A Comparative Human Rights Analysis of the Legal Regulation of Sexual Identity' [2005] *Feminist Legal Studies* 67.

Cowan S., 'Looking Back (To)wards the Body: Medicalization and the GRA' [2009] *Social & Legal Studies* 247.

Craig E., 'Trans-Phobia and the Relational Production of Gender' [2007] *Hastings Women's Law Journal* 137.

Fausto-Sterling A., 'The Five Sexes: Why Male and Female Are Not Enough' [1993] *The Sciences* 20.

Fishbayn L., '"Not Quite One Gender or the Other": Marriage Law and the Containment of Gender Trouble in the United Kingdom' [2007] *Journal of Gender, Social Policy & the Law* 413.

Gilden A., 'Toward a More Transformative Approach: The Limits of Transgender Formal Equality' [2013] *Berkley Journal of Gender, Law & Justice* 83.

Gilmore S., 'The Gender Recognition Act 2004' [2004] *Family Law* 741.

Gonzalez-Salzberg D., ' The Accepted Transsexual and the Absent Transgender: A Queer Reading of the Regulation of Sex/Gender by the European Court of Human Rights' [2014] *American University International Law Review* 797.

Grabham E., 'Governing Permanence: Trans Subjects, Time and the Gender Recognition Act' [2010] *Social & Legal Studies* 107.

Greenberg J., Herald M. and Strasser M., 'Beyond the Binary: What Can Feminists Learn from Intersex Transgender Jurisprudence' [2010] *Michigan Journal of Gender & Law* 13.

Harris A., 'Non-Binary Gender Concepts and the Evolving Legal Treatment of UK Transsexed Individuals: A Practical Consideration of the Possibilities of Butler' [2012] *Journal of International Women's Studies* 57.

Jeffreys S., 'They Know It When They See It: The UK Gender Recognition Act 2004' [2008] *British Journal of Politics & International Relations* 328.

Kogan T., 'Transsexual and Critical Gender Theory: The Possibility of a Restroom Labeled "Other"' [1996-1997] *Hastings Law Journal* 1223.

Lamble S., 'Unknowable Bodies, Unthinkable Sexualities: Lesbian and Transgender Legal Invisibility in the Toronto Women's Bathhouse Raid' [2009] *Social & Legal Studies* 111.

MacNamee E., 'Girls and Boys' [2004] *Law and Critique* 25.

Rellis J., "Please Write 'E' in this Box' Toward Self-Identification and Recognition of a Third Gender: Approaches in the United States and India' [2007-2008] *Michigan Journal of Gender & Law* 223.

Sandland R., 'Feminism and the Gender Recognition Act 2004' [2005] *Feminist Legal Studies* 43.

Sandland R., 'Running to Stand Still' [2009] *Social & Legal Studies* 253.

Sharpe A. N., 'Endless Sex: The Gender Recognition Act 2004 and the Persistence of a Legal Category' [2007] *Feminist Legal Studies* 57.

Sharpe A. N., 'A Critique of the Gender Recognition Act 2004' [2007] *Bioethical Inquiry* 33.

Sharpe A., 'A Return to the 'Truth' of the Past' [2009] Social & Legal Studies 259.

Sharpe A., 'Gender Recognition in the UK: A Great Leap Forward' [2009] *Social & Legal Studies* 241.

Sharpe A., 'Transgender Marriage and the Legal Obligation to Disclose Gender History' [2012] *The Modern Law Review* 33.

Spade D., 'Keynote Address: Trans Law & Politics on a Neoliberal Landscape' [2008-2009] *Temple Political & Civil Rights Law Review* 353.

Tirohl B. and Bowers I.R., 'Opposite Sex – A Discussion of Rights Under the Gender Recognition Act' [2006] *Journal of Gender Studies* 83.

Tirohl B., 'A Study of the Rights of Cross-dressers in the UK' [2007] *Journal of Gender Studies* 277.

Travis M., 'Accommodating Intersexuality in European Union Anti-Discrimination Law' [2014] *European Law Journal* 180.

Vade D., 'Expanding Gender and Expanding the Law: Toward a Social and Legal Conceptualization of Gender That Is More Inclusive of Transgender People' (2004) 11 *Michigan Journal of Gender and Law* 253.

Valdes F., 'Queers, Sissies, Dykes, and Tomboys: Deconstructing the Conflation of "Sex", "Gender" and "Sexual Orientation" in Euro-American Law and Society' [1995] *California Law Review* 1.

Whittle S., 'The Opposite of Sex is Politics – The UK Gender Recognition Act and Why it is Not Perfect, Just Like You and Me' [2006] *Journal of Gender Studies* 267.

Whittle S. and Turner L., "'Sex Changes?' Paradigm Shifts in 'Sex' and 'Gender' Following the Gender Recognition Act?' [2007] *Sociological Research Online* < http://www.socresonline.org.uk/12/1/whittle.html> accessed 10 March 2015.

Reports

International Commission of Jurists (ICJ), *Yogyakarta Principles—Principles on the application of international human rights law in relation to sexual orientation and gender identity*, March 2007.

Internet Sources

Goldberg M., 'What is a Woman?: The Dispute Between Radical Feminism and Transgenderism' (*The New Yorker*, 4 August 2014) <http://www.newyorker.com/magazine/2014/08/04/woman-2> accessed 25 March 2015.

Home Office, 'Transgender Equality' (*The National Archives*) <http://webarchive.nationalarchives.gov.uk/20130128141739/http://homeoffice.gov.uk/equalities/lgbt/transgender-equality/> accessed 20 March 2015.

Aileen McColgan, 'Transgender Discrimination' (Westlaw Insight, 19 February 2014) <http://login.westlaw.co.uk/maf/wluk/app/document?&srguid=i0ad82d080000014cacfe9f470d545744&docguid=I10DB0F00997211E38042969C9A35621A&hitguid=I10DB0F00997211E38042969C9A35621A&rank=2&spos=2&epos=2&td=3&crumb-action=append&context=18&resolvein=true> accessed 20 March 2015.

HM Courts & Tribunals Service, 'Gender Recognition Panel Guidance' (23 December 2014)< https://www.justice.gov.uk/tribunals/gender-recognition-panel> accessed 10 March 2015.

The National Archives, 'Tribunals Service: Gender Recognition Panel' (12 April 2015) < http://webarchive.nationalarchives.gov.uk/20110206182821/http://www.grp.gov.uk/aboutus.htm> accessed 12 April 2015.

Ministry of Justice 'Gender Recognition Certificate Statistics' (*The National Archives,* 24 January2013)<http://webarchive.nationalarchives.gov.uk/20130128141739/http://www.justice.gov.uk/statistics/tribunals/gender-recognition-certificate-statistics> accessed 1 March 2014.

UK Parliament 'Equality Bill Committee Debates-Associated Memoranda' <http://www.publications.parliament.uk/pa/cm200809/cmpublic/cmpbequality.htm#memo> accessed 15 March 2015.

Press for Change Homepage < http://www.pfc.org.uk> accessed 1 March 2015.

Press for Change Homepage, 'Trans Research' <http://www.pfc.org.uk/Research.html> accessed 1 March 2015.

Equality and Human Rights Commission, 'Private and Public Sector Guidance' <http://www.equalityhumanrights.com/private-and-public-sector-guidance> accessed 10 March 2015.

Home Office, 'Lesbian, Gay, Bisexual and Transgender people and the law' (*The National Archives)*<http://webarchive.nationalarchives.gov.uk/20130128141739/http://homeoffice.gov.uk/equalities/lgbt/lgbt-law/> accessed 1 March 2015.

Press for Change Homepage, 'Hate Crime Literature' <http://www.pfc.org.uk/hatecrimerep.html> accessed 14 March 2015.

News Articles

BBC, 'Campaign calls for legal recognition of third gender' (Scotland, 3 November 2014) <http://www.bbc.com/news/uk-scotland-edinburgh-east-fife-29850756> accessed 8 March 2014.

BBC, 'Germany allows 'indeterminate' gender at birth' (1 November 2013) < http://www.bbc.com/news/world-europe-24767225> accessed 10 March 2015.

Davidson H., 'Third gender must be recognised by NSW after Norrie wins legal battle' *The Guardian* (Australia, 2 April 2014) < http://www.theguardian.com/world/2014/apr/02/third-gender-must-be-recognised-by-nsw-after-norrie-wins-legal-battle> accessed 15 March 2015.

Fenton S., 'Are Universities Doing Enough to Support Transgender Students' *The Guardian* (London, 2 February 2015) <http://www.theguardian.com/education/2015/feb/02/are-universities-doing-enough-to-support-transgender-students> accessed 14 March 2015.

Ross E., 'Transgender: Is there still fear in the workplace?' *The Guardian* (London, 5 March 2015) *<http://www.theguardian.com/sustainable-business/2015/mar/05/transgender-fear-workplace-business*> accessed 10 March 2015.

Scobey-Thal J., 'Third Gender: A Short History' *Foreign Policy* (30 June 2014) < http://foreignpolicy.com/2014/06/30/third-gender-a-short-history/ > accessed 15 March 2015.

Young-Powell A. and Page L., 'One in five LGBT students have been bullied or harassed on campus' *The Guardian* (London, 15 May 2014)<http://www.theguardian.com/education/abby-and-libby-blog/2014/may/15/one-in-five-lgbt-students-have-been-bullied-or-harassed-on-campus> accessed 13 March 2015.

Post-*Prest* Corporate Group Veil Piercing: Alternative Avenues to Justice

Charlotte Kouo†

Following the landmark decision of Prest v Petrodel Resources *in 2013, it has been emphasized that it is indeed important to limit corporate veil piercing powers to very carefully defined circumstances. However, because the common law fails to clearly distinguish the circumstances under which corporate veil piercing may occur, there remains a lack of predictability in this area for those seeking justice. Furthermore, there are increased difficulties faced by victims of fraud committed by corporate groups when seeking redress, as frequently judges' hands are tied by the need to respect the doctrines of separate legal personality and privity. It has been a much-debated topic as to whether this lack of responsibility and injustice in the law calls for development of new legal constructions to help victims achieve more practical and fairer outcomes. This paper evaluates and rejects the urgency call for development of new legal constructions and examines alternative avenues of the law that may achieve similar outcomes without requiring the corporate veil to be pierced.*

Keywords: Corporate Veil, Corporate Groups, Limited Liability.

† Charlotte is a final year LLB (Hons) student at the University of Leicester.

1. Introduction

The doctrine of separate legal entity[1] is a fundamental principle of company law, confirmed by the House of Lords in *Salomon v A Salomon & Co Ltd.*[2] Per Lord Halsbury, an incorporated company is to 'be treated like any other independent person with its rights and liabilities appropriate to itself'.[3] Disputably, there exists a discretionary jurisdiction where courts may pierce the corporate veil and potentially investigate parties controlling the entity. While facilitating statute exists,[4] these constraints are beyond the courts' interpretive control. At common law, the standards of veil piercing remain elusively vague causing lack of predictability and commercial uncertainty. Currently, it is problematic for a victim of fraud committed by a corporate group to get redress, as beyond the already restrictive rules of veil piercing, the courts have to circumvent the doctrine of privity.[5] However, because Trust and Tort Law serve as alternatives to hold parties hiding behind the shield of incorporation liable, it is unnecessary to introduce new legal constructions to veil piercing for corporate groups. Courts have consolidated this in recent case law, availing veil piercing as a last resort in carefully defined circumstances.

2. Doctrine of Privity

Often, claimants seeking damages from companies realize they have no assets and are parts of large corporate groups. Courts must then determine if the defendant company is a wholly separate legal entity from its group. In most cases, courts apply the strict *Salomon* principle and do not pierce the corporate veil.[6] Thus, parent companies and shareholders of said companies, who are entitled to participate as members, hold no personal liability. Additionally, although made unwitting creditors by the defendants' negligence, no measures exist to further protect involuntary creditors, such as tort creditors, hence leaving them with the same legal protections as unsecured voluntary creditors,

[1] Doctrine of separate entity first recognized in *R v Arnaud* (1846) 9 Q.B. 806.

[2] [1897] A.C. 22.

[3] Ibid., at 30; also at 50, 'the company is at law a different person from the subscribers to the memorandum.'

[4] ss.213-215 of the Insolvency Act 1986 and s.993 of the Companies Act 2006.

[5] Dignam and Lowry, *Company Law* (8th edn, OUP 2014) 14-17.

[6] Hawke and Hargreaves, 'Corporate Liability: Smoke and Mirrors' (2003) 14 International Company and Commercial Law Review 14, 75.

who hold low priority in insolvency and company asset distribution.[7] Nonetheless, the subsidiary's insurance cover will often protect them.

In *VTB Capital plc v Nutritek International Corp & Others,*[8] the Supreme Court held that there was no basis to pierce the corporate veil and make the controller a party to any contract entered into by the company. In doing so, the Court stood with the doctrine of privity[9] and the principle of separate legal personality. Historically, as in *Antonio Gramsci Shipping Corp & Others v Stepanovs,*[10] courts have permitted claims against the non-party 'puppeteer' who, 'all the time, was pulling the strings'.[11] Though veil piercing is very rare, there have been sporadic successes whereby the effect was, 'not to alter the beneficial ownership of the company's assets: it is simply to provide for such asset to be available in defined circumstances to the claimant'.[12]

3. APPLYING *SALOMON* TO CORPORATE GROUPS

In the context of corporate groups, the doctrine of limited liability and corporate separation can interpose separate legal entities between each company of the corporate group, potentially causing a lack of legal responsibility and injustice.[13] Due to the nature of the often-indispensable principle of limited liability, controlling enterprises are able to hide away from their legal obligations and the jurisdiction where harm has occurred to the victim; hence making litigation against the wrongdoer more difficult. Traditionally, the doctrine assumed owners as persons who had actually required relevant corporate forms to engage in businesses while capping their investment risks; it did not represent situations where one company owned and controlled others.[14] Should the doctrine of limited liability not be circumvented, victims are limited to compensation not exceeding the actual

---

[7] French and others, *Company Law* (32nd edn, OUP 2015) 670-672.

[8] [2013] UKSC 5.

[9] The doctrine of privity confers rights and obligations to only the parties who are privy to the contract.

[10] [2012] BCC 182.

[11] Ibid., per Burton J, para 26.

[12] *Group Seven Ltd v Allied Investment Corp Ltd & Others* [2014] 1 WLR 735, per Hildyard J, para 63.

[13] Muchlinski, 'Limited liability and multinational enterprises: a case for reform?' [2010] 34 Cambridge Journal of Economics 915, 917-918.

[14] Hansmann and Kraakman, 'Toward Unlimited Liability for Corporate Torts' [1991] 100 Yale Law Journal 1879, 1920.

capital assets of the damaging company. Likewise, controlling shareholders also benefit from limited liability to the wrongs done to victims. Hence, victims of companies belonging to greater corporate groups often face significant under-compensation.[15] To address loopholes in the law and help adapt the mechanics of company law to be better suited for the rising modern development of corporate groups, certain situations have been apportioned as circumstances appropriate for corporate veil piercing.

4. PRE-*PREST* BASES

The courts have allocated outlets for corporate groups where the doctrine of separate legal entity may not apply. A summary of exceptions include where the company: operates as a single economic unit, acts as an agent, is a façade/ sham, or when veil piercing would be in the interests of justice.

In *DHN Food Distributors Ltd v Tower Hamlets LBC*[16], Lord Denning justified disregarding the *Salomon* principle when companies operate as a single economic unit. This was later disapproved in *Woolfson v Strathclyde Regional Council*[17] and *Adams v Cape Industries plc.*[18] Lord Justice Slade stated, 'there is no general principle that all companies in a group of companies are to be regarded as one'.[19] Nevertheless, the court will, 'in appropriate circumstances, ignore the distinction in law between members of a group of companies treating them as one [...] whenever justice so demands'.[20] While guidance is given, the circumstances that would be deemed as such are neither defined nor better clarified.

Likewise, the Court may lift the veil if an agency relationship exists. However, this basis is difficult to prove without day-to-day control and express agreements. The decision in *Smith, Stone & Knight Ltd v Birmingham Corp,*[21] that an agency relationship was a question of case-specific facts, was subsequently confirmed in *Adams* and *Yukong Line Ltd v Rendsburg Investments.*[22] As Lord Justice Slade stated, 'there is no presumption that the

[15] Muchlinski, 918-919.
[16] [1976] 3 All ER 462.
[17] (1979) 38 P& CR 521.
[18] [1990] Ch 433.
[19] Ibid., 532.
[20] Ibid.
[21] [1939] 4 All ER 116.
[22] [1998] 1 WLR 294.

subsidiary is the parent company's alter ego'.[23] Similarly, per Justice Toulson, 'the company [is] in law an entity independent of its owner' and to establish agency there is the 'necessary requirement [...] to show that the relationship of agency was intended to be created'.[24] This basis is not necessarily an exception to *Salomon*, but rather an application of the agency principle.

The veil may also be lifted when the company is used as a façade. As held in *Woolfson*, the corporate veil should be upheld unless circumstances show the company is merely a 'façade concealing the true facts'.[25] The Court of Appeal in *Adams* held that a company's structure is a façade when it is used to evade rights through conduct by law that third parties already possessed.[26] This decision confirmed the approach in *Gilford Motor Co v Horne,*[27] where the veil was lifted when the company was used to avoid liabilities for pre-existing duties, and in *Jones v Lipman,*[28] where the company was used to avoid specific performance. More precisely, the company was 'a device and a sham, a mask [...] to avoid recognition by the eye of equity'.[29] Conspicuously, 'sham' terminology is associated with veil piercing. Of great significance is *Trustor AB v Smallbone (No. 2)*[30] where Sir Andrew Morritt V.C. stated:

> 'the court is entitled to pierce the corporate veil and recognize the receipt of the company as that of the individual(s) in control of it if the company was used as a device or façade to conceal the true facts thereby avoiding or concealing any liability of those individuals(s)'.[31]

Further clarification was provided in *Ben Hashem v Ali Shayif,*[32] which expressed that courts have only pierced the veil when the 'company was being used by its controller in an attempt to immunize himself from liability for some wrongdoing which existed entirely *dehors* the company'.[33] Although *Hashem* does not involve parent and subsidiary companies, it distills

---

[23] *Adams v Cape Industries plc* [1990] Ch 433 at 536.

[24] *Yukong Line Ltd v Rendsburg Investments* [1998] 1 WLR 294 at 304.

[25] Ibid., per Lord Keith at 95.

[26] *Adams v Cape Industries plc* [1990] Ch 433 at 543.

[27] [1933] Ch. 935.

[28] [1962] 1 WLR 832.

[29] Ibid., per Russell J at 836.

[30] [2001] 1 WLR 1177.

[31] Ibid., para 22.

[32] *Ben Hashem v Ali Shayif* [2008] EWHC 2380 Fam.

[33] Ibid., para 199.

principles where this basis would apply: where companies were (1) set up to avoid obligations (e.g. *Jones* and *Gilford*) and (2) used to evade consequences of non-performance (e.g. *Trustor*). While this is the only basis regarded as legitimate veil piercing, principles such as those of tort law may be employed to sidestep the corporate veil.

The old law recognized veil piercing in the interests of justice per *Creasy v Breachwood Motors Ltd,*[34] now overruled by *Ord v Belhaven Pubs Ltd,*[35] so as 'to achieve justice where its exercise is necessary for that purpose'.[36] Nonetheless, this approach has been suppressed in several influential Court of Appeal cases and alone remains insufficient to pierce the veil. Per *Adams*, which *Yukong* confirmed, 'the court is not free to disregard the principles of *Salomon* merely because it considers that justice so requires'.[37]

5. Modern Approach

In *Prest v Petrodel Resources*[38] the Supreme Court attempted to introduce and clarify veil piercing. While no significant changes were made, all seven judges accepted that the appeal be allowed and declined to pierce the corporate veil. This follows the normative pre-*Prest* approach in *Adams*—where there is no façade, there will be no veil piercing even if doing so would be in the interests of justice; the mere requisite presence of impropriety does not equate to automatic veil piercing.

However, alongside varying degrees of approval, Lord Sumption categorized existing cases into two principles: 'evasion' and 'concealment'. While these were *obiter*, they present significant contributions. Divined from their Lordships' judgments, the veil can only be pierced through the evasion principle, which applies when a controller has used the company to facilitate evasion of an existing liability; this principle would pertain to cases like *Gilford* and *Jones.* Noting that, 'references to a 'façade' or 'sham' beg too many questions',[39] his Lordship described the concealment principle as, 'the interposition of the company to maintain the pretense that it was being carried

[34] [1992] BCC 638.

[35] [1998] 2 BCLC 447.

[36] *Creasy v Breachwood Motors Ltd* [1992] BCC, per Judge Southward QC at 647.

[37] *Adams v Cape Industries plc* [1990] Ch 433 at 536.

[38] [2013] UKSC 34.

[39] Ibid., para 28.

on by others'.[40] This principle is relevant in cases like *Trustor* and only requires ordinary legal principles to circumvent the corporate veil.

In evasion cases, veil piercing stands as a last resort when no other remedies are available. Although pre-*Prest* cases should be reassessed, it is still relatively unclear when the evasion principle is relevant, as it may not be possible 'to classify all of the cases in which the courts have been or should be prepared to disregard the separate legal personality of a company neatly into cases of either concealment or evasion',[41] and that, 'absent a principle, further development of the law will be difficult for the courts because development of common law and equity is incremental and often by analogical reasoning'.[42]

Due to its open-ended and fact specific nature, the doctrine of corporate veil piercing has received mounting criticism. As Easterbrook and Fischel have put it, piercing the corporate veil 'seems to happen freakishly. Like lightning, it is rare, severe and unprincipled'.[43] Such sentiments have been echoed by many—some academics have since described veil piercing as 'notoriously incoherent [...] and the results unpredictable'[44] and 'unjustifiable, unprincipled, rare and arbitrary',[45] while others have advocated abolition of the doctrine altogether.[46] Likewise, Professor Ballantine observed in 1946 that, 'the formulae invoked usually give no guidance or basis for understanding the results reached'.[47] While it is indeed true that these statements predate *Prest*, the Supreme Court reiterated the above criticisms when delivering their judgment in *Prest*; Lord Neuberger noted that 'the law relating to the doctrine is unsatisfactory and confused'[48] and Lord Walker observed that the doctrine of corporate veil piercing 'is not a doctrine at all in the sense of a coherent principle or rule of law. It is simply a label'.[49]

With corporate veil piercing being faced by a barrage of criticisms, Professor Strasser emerged in defense of the rule, arguing that, if corporate

---

40 Ibid., para 29.

41 *Prest v Petrodel Resources* [2013] 2 AC 415, per Baroness Hale, para 92.

42 *Antonio Gramsci Shipping Corp v Recoletos Ltd & Others* [2014] Bus LR 239, per Beatson LJ, para 66.

43 Easterbrook and Fischel, 'Limited Liability and the Corporation' [1985] 52 University of Chicago Law Review 89, 89.

44 Millon, 'Piercing the Corporate Veil, Financial Responsibility, and the Limits of Limited Liability' [2007] 56(5) Emory Law Journal 1305, 1381.

45 Bainbridge, 'Abolishing Veil Piercing' (July 21, 2000) UCLA School of Law.

46 Ibid.

47 Ballantine, *Ballantine on Corporations* (Callaghan and Co 1946), 312.

48 *Prest v Petrodel Resources* [2013] UKSC 34, para 64.

49 Ibid., para 106.

veil piercing was as flawed as what other academics had made it out to be, it should have and would have been left behind and abandoned long ago.[50]

Hence, since veil piercing has not been expressly abolished and remains only to prevent novel situations of corporate personality abuse, there remain a number of alternative avenues that may better assist victims seeking redress.

6. ALTERNATIVE AVENUES: TRUST LAW

Within *Prest*, an alternative to piercing the corporate veil via trust law was found. On the facts, the Court found that the companies held properties on trust for the husband, making him beneficially entitled. *Prest* illustrates a constructive trust as an equitable remedy to benefit a party deprived of rights due to unjust interference. Although such trust analysis in company law is indeed highly fact specific, it is fruitfully exclusive to the common law jurisdiction.

The principles of trust law may, in more readily justifiable means, resolve evasion or concealment cases via the actual trust or accessory solution. The actual trust solution applies when the device company is regarded as a trustee for its controller, hence rendering the controller liable for misconducts committed in the device company's name, while preserving the controller's liability. This sub-avenue is advantageous as it does not contradict *Salomon* and creates certainty in the law by elucidating applicable scenarios. With reference to existing case law, the actual trust solution would present solutions to evasion cases. Considering *Jones*, the device company would be the trustee for the controller, the agent will not incur personal liability and the trust solution would not conflict with land registration requirements.

The accessory solution is relevant when the device company is liable for knowledge of benefits obtained through the controller's breach of duty and the controller becomes liable for dishonest assistance in the dissipation of said funds from the device company's accounts. This sub-avenue should be employed to resolve 'concealment' cases such as *Trustor* for reasons that both the controller and the device company become liable. Furthermore, having to prove deceit in dishonest assistance claims makes any argument that the accessory solution would open litigation floodgates invalid. Likewise, *FHR European Ventures LLP v Cedar Capital Partners LLC*[51] clarifies that bribes

---

[50] Strasser, 'Piercing the Veil in Corporate Groups' (2005) 37 Connecticut Law Review 637, 650.

[51] [2015] AC 250.

and secret commissions received by an agent should be treated as property of the principal, that the principal has a proprietary remedy against the agent with respect to the bribe itself and cannot give rise to a claim for equitable compensation. This overruled *Sinclair Investments v Versailles*,[52] therefore giving principal priority over creditor claims in the event of the agent's insolvency. Had it not been for *FHR*, the accessory solution would not be able to extend to proprietary relief of the fiduciary's breach of duty.[53]

7. ALTERNATIVE AVENUES: TORT LAW

Many recent developments in veil lifting have incorporated claims in tort law and it is undeniably true that tortious liability is a fault line created through limited liability. As seen in *Chandler v Cape plc,*[54] an asbestos-related case, in applying tort law principles, the parent company was found to have owed direct duty of care to one of its subsidiary company's employees. Through satisfaction of the threefold test of foreseeability, proximity, and fairness, enunciated in *Caparo v Dickman,*[55] the victim was able to seek redress without piercing the corporate veil. Nonetheless, the courts stress that the duty of care is not automatic and is only relevant in specific circumstances, as 'it is not possible to say in all cases what is or is not a normal incident of the relationship between a parent and subsidiary'.[56] *Chandler* identified parallel duties of care between the parent company and its subsidiary employees, and the subsidiary company and the parent company's employees. The parent company (i) and subsidiary company had similar businesses; (ii) ought to have known the subsidiary's work environment was unsafe; and (iii) ought to have foreseen that the subsidiary would rely on them for employee protection. As confirmed in *Thompson v The Renwick Group plc*,[57] Tomlinson LJ expressed that a duty of care will be imposed only where 'it is fair, just and reasonable to impose a duty of a given scope upon the one party for the benefit of another',[58] and that is because a group of companies operating in a single

---

[52] [2011] EWCA Civ 347.

[53] Mcgrath, 'FHR European Ventures LLP: the demise of Sinclair v Versailles and a welcome return to orthodoxy' [2014] 7(5) Corporate Rescue and Insolvency Journal 175, 176.

[54] [2012] EWCA Civ 525.

[55] [1990] 2 AC 605.

[56] *Chandler v Cape plc* [2012] EWCA Civ 525, per Arden LJ, para 67.

[57] [2014] EWCA Civ 635.

[58] Ibid., para 28.

business cannot equate to disrespect for the legal personality of subsidiary companies.

8. CONCLUSION

Piercing the corporate veil is a common law doctrine that is utilized to disregard the *Salomon* corporate personality rule. Evolution of company law has found that in very rare and limited circumstances, where a company's controller abuses the company's separate personality by committing a grave impropriety, the courts may pierce the corporate veil in order to allow a victim to seek redress where there are no other remedies available. This is still the last resort for courts when no other options are available to help the victim appropriately seek redress. Where the law currently stands, it is difficult for a victim of fraud committed by a corporate group to access remedies, as the corporate personality is both legally and economically fundamental to the business world. As a result, judges' hands are often tied by the doctrine of privity in contract law thus putting legal certainty into question. While in recent case law their Lordships have sought to clarify ambiguity as to when exactly the corporate veil may be pierced, there are still no clear lines drawn out for when veil piercing will occur for corporate groups. Nonetheless, it is not absolutely necessary to introduce new legal constructions to piercing the corporate veil, as ordinary legal principles do already help victims seek redress through the alternative avenues of tort law and trusts law.

WORKS CITED

Primary Sources

Legislation

Insolvency Act 1986
Companies Act 2006

Case Law

Adams v Cape Industries plc [1990] Ch. 433
Antonio Gramsci Shipping Corp & Others v Stepanovs [2012] B.C.C. 182

Antonio Gramsci Shipping Corp v Recoletos Ltd & Others [2014] Bus. L.R. 239
Ben Hashem v Ali Shayif [2008] EWHC 2380 Fam
Caparo v Dickman [1990] 2 A.C. 605
Chandler v Cape plc [2012] EWCA Civ 525
Creasy v Breachwood Motors Ltd [1992] B.C.C. 638
DHN Food Distributors Ltd v Tower Hamlets LBC [1976] 3 All ER 462
FHR European Ventures LLP v Cedar Capital Partners LLC [2015] A.C. 50
Gilford Motor Co v Horne [1933] Ch. 935
Group Seven Ltd v Allied Investment Corp Ltd & Others [2014] 1 W.L.R. 735
Jones v Lipman [1962] 1 W.L.R. 832
Ord v Belhaven Pubs Ltd [1998] 2 B.C.L.C. 447
Prest v Petrodel Resources [2013] UKSC 34
R v Arnaud (1846) 9 Q.B. 806
Salomon v A Salomon & Co Ltd [1897] A.C. 22
Sinclair Investments v Versailles [2011] EWCA Civ 347
Smith, Stone & Knight Ltd v Birmingham Corp [1939] 4 All ER 116
Thompson v The Renwick Group plc [2014] EWCA Civ 635

Trustor AB v Smallbone (No. 2) [2001] 1 W.L.R. 1177
VTB Capital plc v Nutritek International Corp & Others [2013] UKSC 5
Woolfson v Strathclyde Regional Council (1979) 38 P. & C.R. 521
Yukong Line Ltd v Rendsburg Investments [1998] 1 W.L.R. 294

Secondary Sources

Books

Alan Dignam and John Lowry, *Company Law* (8th edn, Oxford University Press 2014)
Derek French and others, *Company Law* (32nd edn, Oxford University Press 2015)
Henry Winthrop Ballantine, *Ballantine on Corporations* (Callaghan and Co 1946)

Articles and Essays

David Millon, 'Piercing the Corporate Veil, Financial Responsibility, and the Limits of Limited Liability' [2007] 56(5) *Emory Law Journal*.

Frank H. Easterbrook and Daniel R. Fischel, 'Limited Liability and the Corporation' [1985] 52 *University of Chicago Law Review* 89.

Henry Hansmann and Reinier Kraakman, 'Toward Unlimited Liability for Corporate Torts' [1991] 100 *Yale Law Journal* 1920.

Kurt A. Strasser, 'Piercing the Veil in Corporate Groups' (2005) 37 *Connecticut Law Review* 650

Paul Mcgrath, 'FHR European Ventures LLP: the demise of Sinclair v Versailles and a welcome return to orthodoxy' [2014] 7(5) *Corporate Rescue and Insolvency Journal*

Peter Muchlinski, 'Limited liability and multinational enterprises: a case for reform?' [2010] 34 *Cambridge Journal of Economics*

Neil Hawke and Pamela Hargreaves, 'Corporate Liability: Smoke and Mirrors' (2003) 14 *International Company and Commercial Law Review*

Internet Sources

Stephen Bainbridge, 'Abolishing Veil Piercing' UCLA School of Law (July 21, 2000) [Online].

Retention of Title Clauses: A Key to the *Romalpa* Maze

James Mitchell†

This is a review of the current and on-going controversial scope of retention of title clauses, drawn from a detailed analysis of case law and academic commentary. Provided is a clear summary of the various types of retention of title clauses, the origins of those clauses, and the academic debate that has surrounded each of the clauses. Further, it details the current position of each type of clause, drawing on links between traditional Commercial Law and cases in the Law of Restitution; to draw a conclusion that the retention of title clause is theoretically now certain.

Keywords: *Romalpa*, retention of title clauses, mixed goods clauses, commercial law, proceeds of sale clauses, all monies clauses.

1. Introduction

The *Romalpa*[1] case introduced the use of the 'retention of title (RoT) clause', allowing a seller to maintain ownership of the property until the buyer has paid for it—a vital power if the buyer was to go into liquidation and cannot afford to pay their debts to creditors; allowing sellers to 'trace' the property[2], and (most arguably importantly) reclaim possession of it in priority of all other creditors.[3] Originally, the case of *Romalpa* was predicted to be a

---

† LLB, University of Reading; Tax Trainee at Smith & Williamson.

[1] *Aluminium Industrie Vaasen B.V. v Romalpa Aluminium* [1976] 1 WLR 676.

[2] This type of tracing – retrieving the goods from others—comes from the case of *Re Hallett's Estate* (1880) 13 Ch D 696.

[3] The ability to 'have priority over all other creditors' under an RoT clause is permitted under the Insolvency Act 1986, s251.

revolutionary development in commercial law[4] (with RoT clauses quickly incorporated into statute[5]); however, although often unsatisfactorily, the courts have since distinguished cases from it, making this area of law 'a maze, if not a minefield'.[6] The complication arises as the *Romalpa* case created four types of RoT clauses, namely: Simple, All Monies, Proceeds of Sale, and Mixed Goods.

While it can be said with absolute certainty that a Simple RoT clause is effective, the application of the other types of RoT clauses has been the subject of a great deal of uncertainty, with judgments often lacking foundation or explanation. Even so, recent developments have made this area of law reasonably clear, with it currently being possible to predict the outcome of any case involving an RoT clause, and it can be presumed that All Monies clauses are effective. Further, clauses which seek to trace goods—that have been mixed with other goods in a manufacturing process – is likely to be unenforceable. Clauses which seek to enforce a claim over the proceeds of sale of goods, subject to an RoT clause, will be unenforceable unless those proceeds are kept separate from other funds.

2. THE SIMPLE ROT CLAUSE

Established in the case of *Clough Mill*[7], a Simple RoT clause is applicable. A Simple RoT clause allows a seller to retain proprietary title to goods sold to a buyer, where the goods are identifiable and detachable (without causing damage to the buyer's property). As long as the parties intended a fiduciary relationship[8] to exist between the parties, then no charge can be created over the goods—when 'as a matter of legal theory, a person cannot charge a legal

---

[4] Professor Goode, The Times, 11 May 1977 – 'it is doubtful whether any case decided this century has created a greater impact on the commercial law'.

[5] See: Sale of Goods Act 1979, s17 & 19.

[6] Per Staughton J in *Hendy Lennox Ltd v Grahame Puttick Engines Ltd* [1984] 2 All ER 152, [1984] 1 WLR 485. The case law has also been described as 'difficult', see McKendrick, E, *Contract Law: text, cases, and materials* 5th ed. UK, OUP, 2012.

[7] *Clough Mill Ltd v Geoffrey Martin* [1984] 3 All ER 982, [1985] 1 WLR 111, CA.

[8] Millet LJ, *Bristol & West Building Society v Mothew* [1998] Ch 1, a fiduciary is 'someone who has undertaken to act for or on behalf of another in a particular matter, in circumstances which give rise to a relationship of trust and confidence'. Examples of such relationships are: trustee/beneficiary, doctor/patient, solicitor/client and company director/company.

estate that he does not have'.[9] The significance being, that a charge represents a security interest over goods which must be registered under the Companies Act 2006[10], or will be declared void for non-registration. Consequently, this implies that the seller will have no better claim to the goods than anyone else, even if the charge was registered, then the seller's proprietary right over the goods would still rank lower than other creditors. The decision of *Clough Mill* is therefore of paramount importance in establishing that a Simple RoT clause is not a security interest nor requiring registration, instead enabling the seller to maintain ownership of the goods—without ownership actually transferring to the buyer.

3. THE ALL MONIES ROT CLAUSE

In addition, the case of *Clough Mill* also seems to have established that All Monies RoT clauses are enforceable. All Monies clauses ensure ownership is retained in a number of goods, under any contracts made between the seller and buyer, until full payment is given for all goods. The main criticism of these clauses is that they can be inequitable because the clause allows sellers to reclaim all of the identifiable and detachable goods, which are the subject of a contract, even where the buyer has paid for some of them. As a result, no consideration is given to the buyer for the payment[11], thus making the contract

---

[9] *Abbey National Building Society v Cann* [1991] 1 AC 56, per Lord Oliver, 92. See also A Diamond, *The Reform of the Law of Security Interests* [1988] CLP, W Goodhart, *Clough Mill Ltd v Martin – A Comeback for Romalpa?* [1986] 49 MLR 100 and *Capital Finance Co Ltd v Stokes* [1969] 1 Ch 261. RoT clauses do not fall within the list of charges which must be registered under the Companies Act 2006 (Amendment of Part 25) Regulations 2013, Sch 1, Chapter A1: Registration of Company Charges, Company Charges, 859A(7).

[10] Companies Act 1948, s95 requires charges to be registered, or makes them void. Further, the Companies Act 2006, ss860 & 861 lists charges which must be registered, or be declared void under s874. N.B. 'in practice, it is safest to assume that the same rules as to registration of security interests created by RoT clauses apply to both companies and individuals'; R Christpu, *Drafting Commercial Agreements*, United Kingdom, Sweet & Maxwell, 2013, 799.

[11] Although some academics, argue that there is not a total failure of consideration, 'because the buyer had the use of the goods for a certain time' and the seller foregoes the opportunity cost of not selling to the buyer (MacCormack, *'All Liabilities" Reservation of Title Clauses and Company Charges* (1989) Conv 92, 96; see also RM Goode, *Proprietary Rights and Insolvency in Sales Transactions*, UK, Sweet & Maxwell, 1989, 101 – 'It is, indeed hard to see why an all-moneys retention of title clause should change the character of the agreement, for it is, after all, open to the seller to impose any conditions he wishes for the transfer of ownership to his buyer'), it is clear from the case of *Rowland v Divall* [1932] 2 QB 508, that there is no consideration made, even where the buyer has had some use of the goods.

void.[12] In order to combat this unfairness, the Court of Appeal in *Clough Mill* applied a set-off doctrine [13] – whereby the seller would either refund the buyer any profit they made on the resale of the remaining goods or would only take goods, the value of which, amounted only to the existing debt.[14] Nevertheless, this has been criticised since 'the inference must be that, whenever parties enter into a contract containing an all liabilities reservation of title clause, they intend it to create a charge for the benefit of the seller'[15] as a 'simple debtor-creditor relationship'[16] is created.[17] Furthermore, Goodhart warned that the judgment in *Clough Mill* needs to be read in 'context and as limited to single [such as Simple] contract reservation clauses'.[18] Regardless, the All Monies clause has since been affirmed by *Compaq*[19] and has been given statutory footing, by the Insolvency Act 1986, which requires that 'the sums due to one party shall be set-off against the sums due from the other'.[20] This rule gives justification that 'there is no need to interpret the contract as creating a charge'[21] – as it does not act as a security interest, instead allowing the seller to retain possession under a contractual and fiduciary relationship. Under this relationship, the buyer is required to account to the seller for all of the money,

[12] The Sale of Goods Act 1979, s2(1) defines a contract of sale of goods as: 'a contract by which the seller transfers or agrees to transfer the property in goods to the buyer for a money consideration, called the price'. Where the seller doesn't provide consideration for any price given, then the contract would be void, requiring the seller to return the price to the buyer.
[13] This case was also affirmed by the House of Lords in *Armour v Thyssen Edelstahlwerke AG* [1990] 3 All ER 481, N.B. this is a Scottish case and is merely persuasive, not binding, to English courts.
[14] See further, R Bradgate, *Retention of Title in the House of Lords: Unanswered Questions*, (1991) MLR 54:5, 729-734.
[15] W Goodhart, *Clough Mill Ltd v Martin – A Comeback for Romalpa?* [1986] 49 MLR 98.
[16] P Atiyah, J Adams & H MacQueen, *Atiyah's Sale of Goods,* United Kingdom, Pearson, 2010, 472.
[17] This was the view taken by the judges in the cases of *Re Bond Worth Ltd* [1980] Ch 228 and *Borden (UK) Ltd v Scottish Timber Products Ltd* [1981] Ch 25, in which reservation of title clauses were held to amount to registrable charges, making the RoT clauses ineffective, as they were unregistered.
[18] W Goodhart, *Clough Mill Ltd v Martin – A Comeback for Romalpa?* [1986] 49 MLR 102. N.B. Goodhart did concede that Boreham J had purported to uphold an all-monies clause in another case – *John Snow & Co Ltd v DBG Woodcraft & Co Ltd* [1985] BCLC 54, at 62, but argued that the clause in this case was in fact a single contract RoT clause.
[19] *Compaq Computers Ltd v Abercorn Group Ltd* [1991] BCC 484. Although the RoT clause in this case was considered to be void as an unregistered charge, this was for reason of its being ineffective as a proceeds of sale clause, with the all-monies clause being affirmed by the court; see Christpu 2013, 802.
[20] The Insolvency Act 1986, s323(2), see also the Insolvency Rules 1986, Rule 4.90(2). In *National Westminster Bank Ltd v Halesowen Presswork & Assemblies Ltd* [1972] 2 WLR 455, it was held that set-off in insolvency is mandatory.
[21] R Bradgate, *Retention of Title in the House of Lords: Unanswered Questions*, (1991) MLR 54:5.

or for all of the goods, with the refunding of profits being made by way of statutory obligation, rather than any security interest arising from a debtor-creditor relationship.[22] This statutory justification, coupled with the affirmation of All Monies RoT clauses by the Court of Appeal in *Clough Mill,* and the House of Lords in *Armour*[23] suggests that these types of clauses are probably highly enforceable.

4. MIXED GOODS ROT CLAUSES

Although it is evident that the courts are willing to enforce appropriately worded Simple and All Monies RoT clauses, they will not do so where the goods have been mixed in manufacturing and no longer 'remain separate and identifiable.'[24] It was held in *Re Peachdart*[25] that where the goods have been mixed in the manufacturing process and have lost their identity – judged by 'a question of fact'[26] – or have been irreversibly mixed with other goods, they will no longer be the property of the seller and the RoT clause will be ineffective.[27] Therefore, in allocating title of the new good to the seller it would allow the seller to make a windfall profit on the good if they came to sell it, making it essential that any interest held over the new good is registered as a charge.[28] This argument is weak, as set-off could surely resolve this issue., A more persuasive argument is to allow the seller a proprietary interest in the mixed goods, might be to disadvantage other 'suppliers of raw materials, [who] may have contributed components'.[29] An alternative option might be to impose a tenancy in common, allowing each contributor of the final good to hold an equal share. Such a solution currently exists where the seller's goods cannot be identified, as been mixed or confused in storage.

---

[22] See also the decisions in *Tilley v Bownoti* [1970] 1 KB 745 and *Re Asplrnlric Wood Pavemetif Co* (1885) 30 Ch D 216, which appear to support the availability of set-off in the situation described.

[23] *Armour v Thyssen Edelstahlwerke AG* [1990] 3 All ER 481, N.B. this is a Scottish case and is merely persuasive, not binding, to English courts.

[24] W Goodhart, *Clough Mill Ltd v Martin – A Comeback for Romalpa?* [1986] 49 MLR 96.

[25] *Re Peachdart Ltd* [1984] Ch 131 (Ch). See also *Borden (UK) Ltd v Scottish Timber Products Ltd* [1981] Ch 25, [1979] 3 All ER 961, CA, *Ian Chisolm Textiles Ltd v Griffith* [1994] BCC 96 & commentary by R Bradgate, *Commercial Law*, 3rd ed, UK, LexisNexis UK, 2000, 18.4.2.1 & 18.4.4.

[26] E Baskind, G Osbourne, & L Roach, *Commercial Law*, UK, OUP, 2013.

[27] See W Goodhart, *Clough Mill Ltd v Martin – A Comeback for Romalpa?* [1986] 49 MLR 96.

[28] See R Bradgate, *Commercial Law*, 3rd ed, UK, LexisNexis UK, 2000, (18.4.4) & Christpu 2013, 800.

[29] Bradgate, R, *Commercial Law*, 3rd ed, UK, LexisNexis UK, 2000, 18.4.

Modern rulings have held that the sellers own the mixture as tenants in common, which allows them to recover from it, a quantity equivalent to their input,[30] but only where they can prove that their goods are currently contained in the mixture.[31] This solution was sought, in relation to goods mixed in the manufacturing process, in the case of *Kruppstahl,*[32] where the seller expressly claimed only a proportionate share of the new product. Unfortunately, the Court held that this express admission of holding only a limited interest in the product, in order to secure payment of the debt only, was tantamount to a security interest, creating a charge. Further justification for the Mixed Goods clause is that the courts are reluctant to find a fiduciary relationship as in a bailment:

> 'a person who delivers goods to another, knowing that they will be used in manufacture, must give that other some sort of ownership of them. This prevents a bailment, so that any goods in stock, which have yet to be used in manufacture, cannot be traced. There is no fiduciary relationship'.[33]

Whereas *Hendy Lennox*[34] held that where the goods can be detached from the manufactured product, without any of the goods being damaged, the seller can recover them. In *Aircool*,[35] this was subject to further restriction, such that, 'the seller must have carried out very little work to change or adapt the sub-assembly himself'.[36] However, this qualification only extends to specific cases

[30] See *Indian oil Corporation v Greenstone Shipping SA* [1988] QB 345.

[31] See *Ian Chisolm* [1994] BCC 96. See also RM Goode, *Proprietary Rights and Insolvency in Sales Transactions*, UK, Sweet & Maxwell, 1989, 91 & R Christpu, *Drafting Commercial Agreements*, United Kingdom, Sweet & Maxwell, 2013, 799, who notes that 'in appropriate circumstances, such wrongful intermixture might also produce an equitable remedy under the principles in *Re Hallet's Estate*' and that 'it is also worth noting that where a receiver ignores the provisions of such clauses and continues to deal with goods as if they were not subject to the RoT clause, he will be personally liable ot the true owner under the Tort (Interference With Goods) Act 1977 for their conversion; see *Chaigley Farms* [1996] BCC 957.

[32] *Kruppstahl v Quittman* [1982] ILRM 551.

[33] D Keenan, *Smith and Keenan's Law for Business*. 13th ed, UK, Pearson Longman, UK, 2006, 315.

[34] *Hendy Lennox (Industrial Engines) Ltd v Grahame Puttick Ltd* [1984] 2 All ER 152, [1984] 1 WLR 485.

[35] *Aircool Installations v British Telecommunications PLC* [1995] CLC 95/821 CC (Central London).

[36] See Christpu, 2013, 800-801, where reference is made to the decisions of *Re Peachdart* and *Clough Mill.* Reference is also made to the case of *Aircool Installations v British Telecommunications PLC* [1995] CLC 95/821 CC (Central London), in which air-conditioning equipment, which was subject to an RoT clause, became part of a building, despite it being possible for the seller to detach the good from the building with a certain amount of work.

of land law, where items are deemed to be a fixture to land,[37] with there being no reason to assume that this condition extends further into other types of contract. Therefore, it is currently possible to contemplate that RoT clauses will not be effective, over goods which have been manufactured, unless the original goods can be separated without damage.[38] Moreover, RoT clauses to goods mixed in storage will only be applicable where the clause expressly states that the seller's goods will be stored separately.[39]

5. PROCEEDS OF SALE CLAUSES

The final type of RoT clause, the Proceeds of Sale clause, has been 'particularly vulnerable'[40] to judicial attack with *Romalpa* being 'the only successful example to date'.[41] The main problem with this type of clause has always been that it raises a difficult question of policy, namely, whether to

---

[37] Whilst the question of whether an item is a fixture or not is often uncertain, *Botham and ors v TSB Bank PLC* [1996] EWCA Civ 549, CA listed a number of tests for determining whether something was a fixture or not, including: (i) whether it is intended to be a permanent and lasting improvement, (ii) the practicality of removing the object without damaging the building, (iii) who installed the thing? A builder suggests it is a fixture and fitting, whilst work done by the occupier is less likely to be, (iv) are the items necessary for a room to function? e.g. lights; and, (v) most importantly, it is best if both parties make a contractual promise to one another stating what is a fixture and fitting and what is not.

[38] N.B. De Lacy notes the New Zealand case of *Forest Products* [1992] 3 NZLR 304, which is inconsistent with this finding, in which it was held that 'reducing logs to, *inter alia* , smaller logs, wood chips, bark, etc., were not sufficient acts so as to transfer title to a buyer'. However, he disregards this as 'a decision which must be regarded as doubtful when transposed into the context of current English law'. (J De Lacy, *Retention of Title and Clams Against Processed Goods*, conv. 1998, Jan/Feb).

[39] Christpu, 2013, 799-800 – 'in appropriate circumstances, such wrongful intermixture might also produce an equitable remedy under the principles in *Re Hallet's Estate*' and that 'it is also worth noting that where a receiver ignores the provisions of such clauses and continues to deal with goods as if they were not subject to the RoT clause, he will be personally liable to the true owner under the Tort (Interference With Goods) Act 1977 for their conversion'; see *Chaigley Farms* [1996] BCC 957 QBD.

[40] Bourbon-Select, C. (2005) 20(9), 419-425 JIBLR.

[41] W Davies, *Romalpa thirty years on – still an enigma?* 4(2), HLJ, 5 [accessed online] https://www.herts.ac.uk/__data/assets/pdf_file/0007/38671/HLJ_V4I2_Davies.pdf [06/02/15].

allow a contractual right to give precedence to an unsecured creditor over the rights of other secured creditors.[42]

Following *Compaq*, [43] many now deem the Proceeds of Sale clause to be redundant – very similar to that in *Romalpa;*[44] consequently, the clause was rejected. It is noteworthy that *Compaq* is still distinguishable from *Romalpa.*[45] In *Romalpa,* a fiduciary relationship expressly existed, by the buyer's admission, and impliedly existed, by his paying the proceeds into a separate bank account. Whereas in *Compaq,* the contract expressly stated that no such relationship existed, with the buyer's act of factoring, selling on to a third party the invoices; also impliedly ran contrary to any intention of creating a fiduciary relationship. Therefore, *Compaq* does not preclude the possibility that a Proceeds clause might exist where a fiduciary relationship exists[46], and where the proceeds of the sale are paid into a separate bank account.[47]

5.1.Nemo Dat Quod Non Habet

The rule of s21 Sale of Goods Act 1979—*nemo dat quod non habet*—that a person cannot give what is not theirs to give, solidifies the theoretical underpinning that a buyer cannot sell ownership or legal rights to goods, which are subject to an RoT clause; thereby providing an added protection for the seller. Nevertheless, s25 of the Sale of Goods Act 1979 delivers an exception to the above rule. Essentially holding that the buyer, who is in possession of the goods, is allowed to pass the good title—preventing the

---

[42] Compare, Templeman LJ in *Borden (UK) Ltd* [1981] Ch 25, at 973, who was 'unwilling to imply a term or invoke the aid of equity to produce a result which other creditors of the buyers might justifiably regard as a fraudulent preference', and the view of Goff LJ in *Clough Mill* [1984] 3 All ER 982 that 'I can see no reason why the law should not give effect to that intention' of the parties to create a relationship of bailment. In fact, this area is so subjective and policy-based, that most judges are reluctant even to comment *FG Wilson (Engineering) Ltd v John Holt & Co (Liverpool) Ltd* (CA) [2014] 1 WLR, 26, per Longmore LJ – 'I fear that… I have to refer to at least some of the authority' from *Romalpa.*

[43] *Compaq Computers Ltd v Abercorn Group Ltd* [1991] BCC 484.

[44] Andrew Hicks, *Retention of Tile: Latest Developments* [1992] JBL 398, at 411 – commented 'it is hard to conceive of a seller's claim to proceeds having a better chance of success than this one'. See also de Lacy, J, *Reservation of Title and Charges on Company Book Debts: The Death of Romalpa?* (1991) 54 MLR 736.

[45] See Christpu 2013, 797-798.

[46] Which is to be 'construed in the context of the whole agreement and the surrounding circumstances of the individual case'; see *Compaq Computers Ltd v Abercorn Group Ltd* [1991] BCC 484, at 612, per Mummery J.

[47] In *Re Peachdart Ltd* [1984] Ch 131, a proceeds clause was rejected because proceeds weren't paid into a separate bank account. Though it is unclear why one cannot trace into a mixed fund under the *Agip v Jackson* [1991] Ch 547 principle of equitable tracing.

seller from reclaiming the goods.[48] However, should the sub-buyer have knowledge of the RoT clause[49], and that the original buyer did not have permission to make the sale, then the clause would be ineffective.

Further, in *Fairfax*[50] the Court held that it was a commercial necessity for buyers to have an implicit authority to sell goods to sub-buyers, regardless of any express term that may be of the contrary, and offered protection to a sub-buyer with notice of the RoT clause.[51] Whilst the case has been criticised for allowing an implied clause to 'trump' an express clause, and for failing to take account of earlier possibly contradictory rulings,[52] its application (if not its reasoning) is likely to be applied in future decisions.[53] On this understanding, the effectiveness of the Proceeds of Sale clause is limited for the buyer, as their security is lost once the goods are sold to a sub-buyer. Still, this ability of resale is fundamental to the basis of an RoT clause, as the goods are transferred to the buyer on the condition that they will be paid for upon sale to a sub-buyer – such as when they receive funds.

5.2.The Problem of the Charge

In spite of that, even if a Proceeds of Sale clause were to be upheld, it was considered in *FG Wilson*[54] that Common Law will dictate that 'any trust of the proceeds only applies to the amount which the buyer owes the seller'.[55] Subsequently, this holding is inconsistent with the idea of an agency relationship existing. It is arguable that a buyer should not be entitled to the profits in such an agreement; thus meaning 'that the buyer has created a

---

[48] Millet LJ, *Foskett v McKeown* [2001] 1 AC 102, at [127], 'following is the process of following the same asset as it moves from hand to hand. Tracing is the process of identifying a new asset as the substitute for the old'.

[49] In *Forsythe* [1994] 1 All ER 851, the original seller was able to follow and reclaim their goods from the sub-buyer, as the sub-buyer had notice of the seller's RoT clause. However, where the sub-buyer did not have notice of the original RoT clause, then they will gain good title to the goods, which cannot be followed; see the Sale of Goods Act 1979, ss12 & 25.

[50] *Fairfax Gerrard Holdings Ltd v Capital Bank PLC* [2007] EWCA Civ 1226; [2008] 1 All ER (Comm) 632; [2008] 1 Lloyd's Rep 297.

[51] Ibid at 301. In this case, the court made reference to *Romalpa*, n1 above, and *Four Point Garage Ltd v Carter* [1985] 3 All ER 12.

[52] See *Highway Foods Internation Ltd, Mills v Harris (Wholesale Meat Ltd)* [1995] 1 BCLC 209, [1995] BCC 271.

[53] See S Thomas, *The Role of Authorization in Title Conflicts Involving Retention of Titlce Clauses: Some American Lessons*, (2014) CLWR 43, for full analysis.

[54] *FG Wilson (Engineering) Ltd v John Holt & Co (Liverpool) Ltd* [2014] 1 WLR 2365.

[55] Ibid., 28. See also M Bridge, *Benjamin's Sale of Goods*, 8th ed, UK, Sweet & Maxwell, 2010, 5-153.

registrable charge over the proceeds'.[56] Therefore, for a fiduciary relationship to exist, the RoT clause must apply to the whole proceeds of the sale. Yet in *Welsh Development*, the problem of the charge was successfully avoided by allowing an agency relationship to exist 'even if the principal [the buyer] allows to deduct his commission from the proceeds he collects'.[57] This allowed the seller to recover his debt only and pay the buyer any profit by way of commission. Hence, it is questionable why a Proceeds clause needs to create a charge, when an All Monies clause does not.[58] Nonetheless, this is easily reconciled with the fact that 'a company can create a charge only on its own property, and if it never acquires property in the goods… it cannot charge them'[59] and so cannot create a charge over the goods subject to an RoT, but does acquire property in money paid to it; thus, making proceeds registrable as a charge. Furthermore, a reason why the court may hold that a charge is created is that 'where the buyer is permitted to sub-sell in the normal course of business, he will do so for his own account' [60] and not as a fiduciary. It has been suggested that whilst this might negate the ability of the seller to pursue the proceeds by equitable tracing, 'common law tracing does not require a fiduciary relationship';[61] arguably giving rise to an action in this form. However, the existence of a fiduciary relationship is necessary to prevent the clause creating a security interest and so Common Law tracing would be destined to fail.

5.3.Restitution and the Failure of Consideration – Applying *Quistclose*

A final justification for the Proceeds of Sale clause is that equitable tracing, by way of a fiduciary relationship, should succeed if the relationship was seen as one of bailment[62] – 'where one person is voluntarily in possession of goods that belong to another'.[63] This would allow the seller, where they contracted to

---

[56] *FG Wilson (Engineering) Ltd v John Holt & Co (Liverpool) Ltd* [2014] 1 WLR 2365, 28.
[57] *Welsh Development Agency v Export Finance Co Ltd* [1992] BCLC 149. See Christpu 2013, 798-799.
[58] See G McCormack, *Registration of Company Charges*, 2nd ed, (2005), Jordans, 174.
[59] P Atiyah, J Adams & H MacQueen, *Atiyah's Sale of Goods,* United Kingdom, Pearson, 2010, 470.
[60] *Pfeiffer Weinkellerei-Weineinkauf GmbH & Co v Arbuthnot Factors Ltd* [1988] 1 WLR 150, at 159.
[61] W Davies, *Romalpa thirty years on – still an enigma?* 4(2), HLJ, 7 [accessed online] https://www.herts.ac.uk/__data/assets/pdf_file/0007/38671/HLJ_V4I2_Davies.pdf [06/02/15].
[62] Goff LJ stated in *Clough Mill Ltd v Geoffrey Martin* [1984] 3 All ER 982, [1985] 1 WLR 111, CA, at 116, that he saw no reason why the parties intentions as to a bailee relationship allowing tracing of proceeds should not be allowed.
[63] E McKendrick, *Contract Law: Text, Cases, and Materials.* 5th ed., UK, OUP, 2012, 990.

'retain beneficial interest… (without any explicit contractual clauses extending their claim to proceeds or products) [to] be able to trace (in equity) their beneficial interests in the original goods into proceeds or product'[64] where the buyer sold the goods subject to a limitation on sale. This situation currently exists in the case of a *Quistclose*[65] trust, which exists to bring restitution to the claimant for a failure of consideration that has arisen due to their payment not being used for the purpose that it is specified to be used for. Unfortunately, the justification of the use of a *Quistclose* trust when applying to a Proceeds of Sale RoT clause is not likely when it would require the courts to overturn the decision of the High Court ruling in *Bond Worth*.[66] Even so, the rationale of the *Quistclose* trust can be used to explain the courts current position on Proceeds of Sale RoT clauses. To illustrate this, it is important to note that in *Re Goldcorp*,[67] the 'privy council was at pains to clarify that the money paid by the 'unallocated claimants' fell within the general fund of the defendant's assets and did not have to be applied for a special designated purpose',[68] thus preventing the claimant from reclaiming the funds. Similarly, in Proceeds of Sale RoT clauses, cases have shown that the claimant can only trace funds where they have been allocated for a specific purpose; that is, kept in a separate bank account, for the purpose of repaying the original buyers debt to the original seller. In contrast, where the proceeds have not been kept in a separate bank account, they cannot be reclaimed, as they enter the general fund. This suggests that Proceeds of Sale RoT clauses only apply where the funds have been kept separate, as was the case in *Romalpa* originally; which, in the authors opinion is equitable if you employ the reasoning of the House of Lords in *Westdeutsche*[69]—that the claimant has, after all, 'entered into a commercial transaction, and so has taken the risk of the defendant's insolvency, just like the defendant's other creditors who contracted with it'.[70]

[64] Kelry C.F. Loi, *Quistclose trusts and Romalpa clauses: substance and nemo dat in corporate insolvency* (2012) LQR, 417.
[65] See *Barclays Bank v Quistclose Investments Ltd* [1968] UKHL 4.
[66] *Re Bond Worth Ltd* [1980] Ch 228, where it was held that a seller had to retain legal title as well as equitable title.
[67] *Re Goldcorp Exchange Ltd* [1995] 1 AC 74, 101.
[68] A Burrows, *The Law of Restitution*, New York, Oxford University Press, 2011.
[69] *Westdeutsche Lanedbank Girozentrale v Islington London Borough Council* [1996] AC 669.
[70] Ibid., 683-684.

6. CONCLUSION

It is possible to conclude that Bradgate was right when he wrote that although, strictly speaking, '*Romalpa* remains good law and authority for the proposition that an unpaid seller may be able to trace into proceeds of sale of the goods… subsequent decisions have distinguished *Romalpa* all but out of existence… [even if] the grounds on which they have done so are often unconvincing'.[71] If a Proceeds of Sale clause is to succeed, then it is likely to only be able to do so, where the buyer pays the profits from any subsale into a separate bank account for the original seller. It is advisable that when drafting an RoT clause, claims to proceeds and manufactured goods are drafted in a separate clause, from Simple and All Monies RoT clauses, which appear currently to be applicable; as Proceeds clauses are unlikely to be upheld by the courts, even when drafted well.[72]

WORKS CITED

Primary Sources

Legislation

Companies Act 1948
Companies Act 2006
Companies Act 2006 (Amendment of Part 25) Regulations 2013
Insolvency Act 1986
Insolvency Rules 1986
Sale of Goods Act 1979
Tort (Interference With Goods) Act 1977

Case Law

Abbey National Building Society v Cann [1991] 1 AC 56.
Agip v Jackson [1991](Ch) 547.

[71] R Bradgate, *Commercial Law*, 3rd ed, UK, LexisNexis UK, 2000, 18.4.5.

[72] Although a proceeds clause was upheld in the Australian High Court in *Associated Alloys Pty Ltd v Metropolitan Engineering & Fabrications Pty Ltd* (2000) 171 ALR 568, 'the use of a 'trust' clause in this way would almost certainly be deemed to operate by way of charge security' in English law; J de Lacy, *Corporate Insolvency and Retention of Title Clauses: Development s in Australia* (2001) IL. 70.

Aircool Installations v British Telecommunications PLC [1995] CLC 95/821 CC (Central London).
Aluminium Industrie Vaasen B.V. v Romalpa Aluminium [1976] 1 WLR 676.
Armour v Thyssen Edelstahlwerke AG [1990] 3 All ER 481.
Associated Alloys Pty Ltd v Metropolitan Engineering & Fabrications Pty Ltd (2000) 171 ALR 568.
Barclays Bank v Quistclose Investments Ltd [1968] UKHL 4.
Borden (UK) Ltd v Scottish Timber Products Ltd [1981] (Ch) 25.
Bristol & West Building Society v Mothew [1998] (Ch) 1.
Capital Finance Co Ltd v Stokes [1969] 1 (Ch) 261.
Chaigley Farms Ltd v Crawford Kaye & Grayshire [1996] BCC 957.
Clough Mill Ltd v Geoffrey Martin [1984] 3 All ER 982, [1985] 1 WLR 111, CA.
Compaq Computers Ltd v Abercorn Group Ltd [1991] BCC 484.
Fairfax Gerrard Holdings Ltd v Capital Bank PLC [2007] EWCA Civ 1226.
FG Wilson (Engineering) Ltd v John Holt & Co (Liverpool) Ltd (CA)[2014] 1 WLR.
Forest Products Ltd v Pongakawa Sawmill Ltd [1992] 3 NZLR 304.
Forsythe v Silver Shipping Co Ltd, The Saetta [1994] 1 All ER 851.
Four Point Garage Ltd v Carter [1985] 3 All ER 12.
Hendy Lennox Ltd v Grahame Puttick Engines Ltd [1984] 2 All ER 152, [1984] 1 WLR 485.
Highway Foods Internation Ltd, Mills v Harris (Wholesale Meat Ltd) [1995] 1 BCLC 209, [1995] BCC 271.
Ian Chisolm Textiles Ltd v Griffith [1994] BCC 96.
Indian oil Corporation v Greenstone Shipping SA [1988] (QB) 345.
John Snow & Co Ltd v DBG Woodcraft & Co Ltd [1985] BCLC 54.
Kruppstahl v Quittman [1982] ILRM 551.
National Westminster Bank Ltd v Halesowen Presswork & Assemblies Ltd [1972] 2 WLR 455.
Re Asplrnlric Wood Pavemetif Co (1885) 30 (Ch) D 216.
Re Bond Worth Ltd [1980] (Ch) 228.
Re Goldcorp Exchange Ltd [1995] 1 AC 74.
Re Hallett's Estate (1880) 13 (Ch) D 696.
Re Peachdart Ltd [1984] (Ch) 131.
Rowland v Divall [1932] 2 (QB) 508.
Tilley v Bownoti [1970] 1 (KB) 745.
Westdeutsche Landebank Girozentrale v Islington London BC [1996] AC 669.

Reports

Bourbon-Select, C. (2005) 20(9), 419-425 JIBLR.

Secondary Sources

Books

Atiyah, P, Adams, J, & MacQueen, H, *Atiyah's Sale of Goods,* United Kingdom (Pearson 2010).

Baskind, E, G Osbourne, & L Roach, *Commercial Law*, UK (Oxford University Press 2013).

Bridge, M, *Benjamin's Sale of Goods*, 8th ed, UK (Sweet & Maxwell 2010).

Bradgate, R, *Commercial Law*, 3rd ed, UK (LexisNexis UK 2000).

Burrows, A, *The Law of Restitution*, New York (Oxford University Press 2011).

Christpu, R, *Drafting Commercial Agreements*, United Kingdom (Sweet & Maxwell 2013).

Goode, RM, *Proprietary Rights and Insolvency in Sales Transactions*, UK (Sweet & Maxwell 1989).

Keenan, D, *Smith and Keenan's Law for Business*. 13th ed, UK (Pearson Longman UK 2006).

McKendrick, E, *Contract Law: text, cases, and materials* 5th ed. UK (Oxford University Press 2012).

Articles and Essays

Bradgate, R, *Retention of Title in the House of Lords: Unanswered Questions*, (1991) MLR 54:5.

Davies, W, *Romalpa thirty years on – still an enigma?* 4(2), HLJ, 5 [accessed online] https://www.herts.ac.uk/__data/assets/pdf_file/0007/38671/HLJ_V4I2_Davies.pdf [06/02/15].

de Lacy, J *Corporate Insolvency and Retention of Title Clauses: Development s in Australia,* Insolv. L. 2001, 2(May).

de Lacy, J, *Processed Goods and Retention of Title Clauses*, P.I.C. 1997, 10(Nov), 1-2.

de Lacy, J, *Reservation of Title and Charges on Company Book Debts: The Death of Romalpa?* MLR (1991) 54(5) 736.

de Lacy, J, *Retention of Title and Clams Against Processed Goods*, Conv. 1998, Jan/Feb.

Diamond A. *The Reform of the Law of Security Interests* [1988] CLP.
Goodhart, W, *Clough Mill Ltd v Martin – A Comeback for Romalpa?* [1986] 49 MLR.
Hicks, A, *Retention of Tile: Latest Developments* [1992] JBL 398.
Hicks, A, *Romalpa is Dead* [1992] Comp. Law. 1992, 13(11).
MacCormack, *"All Liabilities" Reservation of Title Clauses and Company Charges* (1989) Conv 92.
Sean Thomas, *The Role of Authorization in Title Conflicts Involving Retention of Titlce Clauses: Some American Lessons*, (2014) CLWR 43

Why Blurring is a Conceptually Difficult Area of Trademark Law

Saquib Rahman†

Abstract: *US Courts have either preferred to address dilution-by-blurring as trademark infringement, or have involuntarily misunderstood the concept as infringement in the past. Even upon recognition of 'blurring' as a separate claim, decisions of the courts with regards to the determination of dilution-by-blurring have differed from one another. Alongside the definition of blurring, this paper critically evaluates how blurring has become a conceptually difficult area of trademark law. Although the latest revision law in the US is believed to have immensely contributed to the better understanding of blurring, this paper identifies certain areas, addressing which would better conceptualize dilution-by-blurring.*

Keywords: Trademarks, Trademark dilution, Dilution-by-blurring, Intellectual property law.

1. EXPLORING DILUTION-BY-BLURRING

Symbols or words are traditionally trademarks when individuals or corporations use them for the purpose of identifying or differentiating their

† LLM (International Corporate Governance & Financial Regulation), University of Warwick; Lecturer of Law at the University of Asia Pacific in Bangladesh.

goods or services.[1] In modern times, however, slogans[2], colours[3], smells[4], shapes[5], sounds[6], gestures, and even taste may be trademarked.[7] In simple words, a customer is helped to classify a product or service (the exact quality of which they are in need of) by the indication of a unique trademark on such product or service.[8] By giving exclusive right to a mark's owner to use the mark for identifying products or services, trademark acts as protection towards the owner of the mark.[9] While laws have been passed for the protection of trademarks considering marketable value, trademark doctrine has significantly developed for the prevention of trademark infringement. However, remedies for dilution have lacked importance.[10] Focusing on "blurring" (a type of dilution), this paper provides two points of consideration to address why it is a conceptually difficult area of trademark law: (1) different standards and factors are considered by courts in order to determine blurring and there are widely varying decisions before and after the enactment of the Federal Trademark Dilution Act 1995, and (2) courts tend to address dilution claims as infringement, although it is altogether a separate claim.

Part (2) below explains what dilution is, defining dilution-by-blurring. In an attempt to address why it is a conceptually difficult area, Part (3) mentions legal standards provided in the Federal Trademark Dilution Act 1995 in order to claim dilution. Part (4) then talks about a split among the courts in interpreting the Act and the factors set by various courts in order to determine dilution-by-blurring. Part (5) states the effect of amendments made to the Act in 2006, and whether they could help conceptualize blurring better. Part (6) aims at answering why blurring is a conceptually difficult area since it is often

---

1 Lynda Oswald, '"Tarnishment" and "Blurring" under the Federal Trademark Dilution Act of 1995' (1999) 36 *American Business Law Journal*, 255, 255.

2 Andrew Terry and Chloe Chittock, 'Shapes And Slogans As Trade Marks: Developments In Case Law' (2010) 18 *Journal of Brand Management* 174, 175.

3 Samuel Londesborough, 'Should Colours Be Protected By Trade Mark Law? What Problems May Arise In Protecting Them?' (Undergraduate, University of Kent) 18.

4 Lee Burgunder, 'Trademark Protection of Smells: Sense Or Nonsense' (1991) 29 *Am Business Law Journal* 459, 462.

5 Terry and Chittock, 176.

6 Matthew Lance Cole, *The Complete Guide To Patents, Copyrights, And Trademarks*(Atlantic Pub Group 2008), 146.

7 Emine Saner, 'You Can't Trademark Everything' (*The Guardian*, 2013) <http://www.theguardian.com/law/shortcuts/2013/jun/04/you-cant-trademark-everything-chanel> accessed 16 April 2015.

8 Wolfgang Sakulin, *Trademark Protection And Freedom Of Expression* (Kluwer Law International 2011), 46.

9 World Intellectual Property Organization (WIPO), *About Trademarks* (2015) <http://www.wipo.int/trademarks/en/about_trademarks.html#function> accessed 16 April 2015.

10 Kathleen McCabe, 'Dilution-By-Blurring: A Theory Caught In The Shadow Of Trademark Infringement' (1999) 68 *Fordham Law Review* 1827, 1828.

confused with trademark infringement, and lastly, prior to conclusion, Part (7) provides certain recommendations. This paper addresses the question mainly in the context of the United States of America.

2. THE CONCEPT OF 'DILUTION' AND EXTRACTING 'BLURRING'

Taking into consideration the *Zinn v. Seruga* case of 2009 in the United States, diminishing the capacity of a well-known mark for the purpose of identifying and distinguishing goods or services is known as Trademark Dilution.[11] Lessening the uniqueness of such a mark occurs in two possible circumstances – (1) when there is presence or even absence of competitiveness between the one owning the well-known mark (original or senior user) and the one using it later (junior user), (2) when there is absence or presence of the likelihood of mistake, confusion or deception.[12] Thomas McCarthy in his book[13] has mentioned that a trademark dilution can be said to occur at instances when any company or individual uses a mark that is either the same or significantly similar to a mark that has already been in existence, activating minds of the consumers[14] to somehow relate between both the marks. Thus, the strength of the original mark wears out.[15] In the case of the 'Kodak bicycle' for instance, irrespective of the fact that most consumers are unlikely to think that the famous company now has a branch or got involved with the bicycle business, and although customers are well aware that the source of Kodak bicycle is different, it would lessen the image of Kodak being solely associated with film.[16] Therefore, it is eroding the strength of the Kodak film company, since customers may think of Kodak film when they see Kodak, or may think of the bicycles. Moreover, in the recent past, selling of "perfumebay", "perfume-bay" or "PerfumeBay" over the internet has been mentioned to dilute the famous shopping site "eBay".[17] Not just the consumers are protected from

---

[11] *Zinn v Seruga* [2009] Civ No 05-3572 (District Court New York).
[12] Ibid.
[13] J. Thomas McCarthy, *Trademarks And Unfair Competition* (Lawyers Co-operative Pub Co 1984).
[14] Krista Holt and Scot Duvall, 'Chasing Moseley's Ghost: Dilution Surveys Under The Trademark Dilution Revision Act' (2008) 98 *The Law Journal of the International Trademark Association* 1311, 1329-1330.
[15] McCabe, 1829.
[16] Kenneth Port, 'Trademark Dilution In Japan' (2006) 4 *Northwestern Journal of Technology and Intellectual Property* 228.
[17] *Perfumebaycom Inc v eBay, Inc* [2007] 506 F3d (9th Circuit).

confusion (as in infringement matters); the theory of dilution protects the worth of the trademark to the holder of such.[18]

Professor Frank I. Schechter, the introducer of dilution law, has defined the harm done by "blurring" in his publication[19] as the "gradual whittling away or dispersion of the identity and hold upon the public mind of the mark or name".[20] The consumers' strong association of a particular mark is blurred since the mark's association is now being shared between two goods. Whenever the unique identity of a particular mark is weakened over its use on goods that are not similar, dilution by blurring occurs.[21] A wiser view is that the usage of a mark on a competing product dilutes that mark as much as usage of such mark on a non-competing product.[22] It is anticipated that the original trademark holder, especially in the case of dilution by blurring, suffers "death by a thousand cuts" over time.[23] As in Kodak's example above, blurring would occur provided the trademark "Dupont" is used for shoes, "Buick" used for aspirin[24] and so on. According to Barton Beebe, "the beauty of the blurring theory of dilution is that it is emphatically empirical in orientation".[25] The scholar further mentioned that in order to discover that a mark blurs another, it is upon the judge to find out that the other user's mark is truly making customers to "think for a moment" prior to recognizing that the original mark refers to the products of the owner of original mark.[26]

"Tarnishment" is the other form of dilution. It concerns an unsanctioned usage of a particular mark that exposes the mark in an objectionable manner, likely to put forward uncomplimentary thoughts regarding the product of the

---

[18] Oswald, 258-260.

[19] Frank I. Schechter, 'The Rational Basis of Trademark Protection' (1927) 40 *Harvard Law Review*, 813, 825.

[20] Matthew D. Bunker and Kim Bissell, 'Lost In The Semiotic Maze: Empirical Approaches To Proof Of Blurring In Trademark Dilution Law' (2013) 18 *Communication Law and Policy* 375, 376.

[21] Alexandra Olson, 'Dilution By Tarnishment: An Unworkable Cause Of Action In Cases Of Artistic Expression' (2012) 53 *Boston College Law Review* 693, 696-697 <http://lawdigitalcommons.bc.edu/cgi/viewcontent.cgi?article=3218&context=bclr> accessed 26 March 2015.

[22] Oswald, 261.

[23] Howard Handelman, *Guide To Trademark Trial And Appeal Board Practice* (Aspen Publishers Online 2007), 8-223.

[24] *Sally Gee, Inc v Myra Hogan, Inc* [1983] 699 F2d (2nd Circuit).

[25] Barton Beebe, 'A Defense Of The New Federal Trademark Antidilution Law' (2006) 16 Fordham Intellectual Property, Media and Entertainment Law Journal, 1142, 1149. <http://ir.lawnet.fordham.edu/cgi/viewcontent.cgi?article=1363&context=iplj> accessed 26 March 2015.

[26] Ibid.

owner, thereby tarnishing goodwill investment made in the owner's mark.[27] Distributers of a well-known counterculture poster were sued by Coca-Cola Company when a poster wrote "Enjoy Cocaine" in the same font as Coca-Cola, making it look like a Coke ad.[28] This paper, however, shall only take into consideration dilution-by-blurring.

3. RELEVANT LEGAL STANDARDS UNDER THE FEDERAL TRADEMARK DILUTION ACT 1995

Courts, prior to the enactment of the Federal Trademark Dilution Act 1995, were reluctant to address dilution claims due to the fear that the decisions could give trademark owners a monopoly on their marks, affecting free competition.[29] It is notable that the Dilution Act's purpose is protecting the "selling power" of the mark,[30] meaning that dilution law only comes into application when the original mark is distinctive enough. Taking effect dated January 16, 1996, an amendment in Section 25 of the Lamham Act was made by the Act – giving "famous" trademarks' owners a federal remedy for dilution. The Act defines dilution as the lessening of the capacity of a famous mark to identify and distinguish goods or services, regardless of the presence or absence of (1) competition between the owner of the famous mark and other parties, or (2) likelihood of confusion, mistake, or deception.[31]

For the purpose of determining (for courts' consideration) if a mark is famous and unique, as many as eight factors were provided: the amount of in-built or attained uniqueness of the mark, the time and degree of use of the mark in relation with the products or services with which the concerned mark is used, the time period and level of advertising and publicity of such mark, geographical range of the business area where the concerned mark is used, the networks of business for products or services with which such mark is used, extent of acknowledgement for the mark in the transaction areas and channels of trade used by such mark's owner and individual against whom injunction is sought, the kind and amount of use of identical or similar marks by other third

---

[27] Alexandra Olson, 'Dilution By Tarnishment: An Unworkable Cause Of Action In Cases Of Artistic Expression' (2012) 53 *Boston College Law Review* 693, 697.
[28] Paul Siegel, *Communication Law In America* (4th edn, Rowman & Littlefield 2014), 257.
[29] Megan Gray, 'Defending Against A Dilution Claim: A Practitioner's Guide' (1996) 205 *Texas Intellectual Property Law Journal*, 206, 220.
[30] Jonathan Mermin, 'Interpreting The Federal Trademark Dilution Act Of 1995: The Logic Of The Actual Dilution Requirement' (2001) 42 *Boston College Law Review* 207.
[31] The Federal Trademark Dilution Act, 1995 ("FTDA").

parties, and lastly, whether the mark was registered in accordance with federal law.[32]

The initial requirements of the Act were quite direct – burden on the plaintiff in establishing that it possesses a famous mark, the other party (defendant) is involved with commercial usage of such mark, other party's adoption of the mark after the original had become famous and lastly, weakening the capacity of the mark to identify and differentiate products and services, the other party's mark dilutes the original.[33] The last element created a split between Circuits (discussed in next Part of this paper). The Act granted injunctive relief and damages or profits in the circumstances of wilful violation, as well as destruction of items that were offensive.[34]

4. Varying Factors and Decisions Made By Courts in Determining Dilution-by-Blurring

The original user is required to display that another's usage causes dilution of the distinguishing quality of the original mark—as mentioned above, courts in the past were divided in this regard. Two Circuits required the original owner to provide evidence of actual economic loss incurred due to usage of the mark by another, causing dilution.[35] On the other hand, four Circuits found it necessary to simply portray a "likelihood of dilution" that may be concluded from certain contextual factors.[36]

4.1.Actual Dilution

Taking into consideration the case of "actual dilution" at first, it has been clarified by the Fourth Circuit (as well as recognized by the Fifth Circuit)[37] that dilution in accordance to the Federal Trademark Dilution Act necessitates evidence of an adequate resemblance between the junior and original marks in

[32] Jon Marans, '*Westchester Media Co. L.P., et al. v PRL USA Holdings, Inc.*: The Fight Over The Name, POLO' (2002) 8 *Jeffrey S. Moorad Sports Law Journal*, 351, 361.
[33] *Panavision Int'l, LP v Toeppen* [1998] 141 F3d (9th Circuit).
[34] FTDA.
[35] *Westchester Media Co, LP v PRL USA Holdings, Inc* [2000] 214 F3d (5th Circuit).
[36] Sid Leach, 'The Federal Trademark Dilution Act Of 1995 Has Not Brought Uniformity And Consistency To The Protection Of Famous Marks' (*Snell & Wilmer*, 2002) <http://www.swlaw.com/assets/pdf/publications/2002/11/09/Trademark-Dilution-by-Sid-Leach.pdf> accessed 28 March 2015.
[37] Christopher Micheletti and Dan Dorfman, 'Proving Dilution By Blurring: An Analysis Of Dilution By Blurring Factors Under The Federal Trademark Dilution Act' (2002) 92 *Official Journal of the International Trademark Association* 1345, 1377.

evoking 'instinctive mental association' of both by an appropriate universe of customers which is the effective reason of an actual diminishing of the original mark's selling power, stated as "its capacity to identify and distinguish goods or services".[38]In the case of *Ringling Bros-Barnum & Bailey Combined Shows, Inc. v. Utah Div Of Travel Dev*, the Fourth Circuit, for the purpose of evidencing actual and consummated dilution of the mark and the reason for such,[39] recognized: (1) "an actual loss of revenues, and proof of replicating use as cause by disproving other possible causes"; and (2) results of a "skillfully constructed consumer survey designed not just to demonstrate 'mental association' of marks in isolation, but further consumer impressions from which actual harm and cause might rationally be inferred".[40] Moreover, the Fourth Circuit specified that courts may take into account suitable factors like the publicity of the other party's mark, the resemblance of the marks and the firmness of the original mark's grip. However, such consideration by courts should only be for the purpose of complementing the evidence shown by actual economic harms and/or proof of survey of actual dilution.[41]

4.2.Likelihood of Dilution

In contrast, for the purpose of taking into concern dilution by blurring claims, appellate courts examined and identified an extensive range of factors (along with appropriate proof), applying the likelihood of dilution standard. There are six factors (commonly termed as the "*Mead Data Central* factors") used prior to the enactment of the Federal Trademark Dilution Act in order to determine likelihood of dilution: resemblance of the marks, resemblance of goods covered by the marks, the customers' sophistication, predatory intention, renown of original mark, and how well the junior mark is known.[42] These are derived from the opinion of Judge Sweet while interpreting the anti-dilution statute of New York, in the case of *Mead Data Central, Inc. v. Toyota Motor Sales, U.S.A., Inc.*[43]

---

[38] Matthew Voss, 'Ringling *Bros.-Barnum & Bailey Combined Shows, Inc. V. Utah Division Of Travel Development & Nabisco, Inc. V. PF Brands, Inc.*' (2000) 15 *Berkeley Technology Law Journal* 265, 273.
[39] Leach, 1.
[40] Micheletti and Dorfman, 1377.
[41] Ibid.
[42] Simon Ilanah, 'The Actual Dilution Requirement In The United States, United Kingdom And European Union: A Comparative Analysis' (2006) 12 *Boston University Journal of Science and Technology Law* 271, 276.
[43] *Mead Data Central v Toyota Motor Sales* [1988] 702 F Supp (District Court Southern District of New York) 1031.

4.3.Criticism of the Likelihood

It is to be noted that several courts applied most (if not all) of the *Mead Data Central* factors after the Federal Act was enacted, while addressing claims of dilution-by-blurring in accordance to the Act, with an exception of the First and Seventh Circuits.

For the purpose of evaluating federal dilution claims, these two circuits discarded the majority of the aforementioned factors.[44] Commonly, certain factors have been rejected by those courts, their argument being that the factors are most likely to be used in the case of likelihood of confusion (which is how trademark infringement is considered) rather than likelihood of dilution.

4.4.The *Nabisco* Case

The Second Circuit implemented the most wide-ranging "nonexclusive list" in the case of *Nabisco, Inc. v. PF Brands, Inc* in order to determine whether dilution by blurring is possible to occur: "(1) distinctiveness; (2) similarity of the marks; (3) proximity of the products; (4) interrelationship among the distinctiveness, similarity, and proximity; (5) shared consumers and geographic limitations; (6) sophistication of consumers; (7) actual confusion; (8) referential quality of the junior use; (9) harm to the junior user and delay by the senior user; and (10) the effect of the senior's prior failure to protect its mark."[45]

On the other hand, the Third Circuit chose to approve of the district court's application of the *Mead Data Central* factors in the case of *Times Mirror Magazines, Inc. v. Las Vegas Sporting News, L.L.C.* The court applied none of the extra factors mentioned in *Nabisco, Inc. v. PF Brands*; however, it mentioned that it had assessed the dilution factors from what Judge Sweet had said, as enhanced in the *Nabisco* analysis.[46]

Moreover, the Sixth Circuit in the *V Secret Catalogue, Inc. v. Moseley* case, emphasized the distinctiveness of the original mark, resemblance between the marks, and the mental association that consumers had the possibility of making between the marks – taking into consideration the

[44] Micheletti and Dorfman, 1349.

[45] Vapnyar Vadim, 'Moseley V. Secret Catalogue, Inc.: Redefining The Scope Of The Federal Trademark Dilution Act' (2012) 77 *St. John's Law Review* 675, 687.

[46] *Times Mirror Magazines, Inc v Las Vegas Sports News, LLC* [2000] 212 F3d (3rd Circuit).

Second Circuit's approach, while not completely disregarding the factors mentioned in the *Nabisco* case.[47]

4.5.Other views

Many courts have not applied broad lists of factors. Stating that factors mentioned in both *Nabisco* and the *Mead Data Central* were more suitable to the likelihood of confusion analysis previously mentioned, the Seventh Circuit rejected both factors in the case of *Eli Lilly &Co. v. Natural Answers, Inc.*[48] Resemblance of the marks and how well known the original mark is were the only two necessary considerations that the Seventh Circuit made. However, an issue was raised in case of *Hasbro, Inc. v. Clue Computing, Inc.* which quoted that, for the purpose of showing dilution; more than two factors (stated by Judge Sweet) must be taken into concern.[49]

The renown of the original mark and the similarity between the marks are two factors mentioned by Judge Sweet that the United States Patent and Trademark Office Trademark Trial and Appeal Board (TTAB) took into consideration. However, it added a factor "whether target customers are likely to associate two different products with the mark even if they are not confused as to the different origins of these products".[50] Just like scholar Thomas McCarthy and two Circuits (First and Seventh), the *Mead Data Central* test was discarded by the TTAB.[51]

In light of the above, it is evident that the varying approaches of the courts (from both splits, "actual dilution" and otherwise) in determining dilution by blurring (including interpretation of the Act over time) have made blurring a conceptually difficult area. However, revision brought in by the 2006 Act (as discussed in the next Part) has taken care of the matter to a great extent.

5. CHANGES IN THE ACT

The Trademark Dilution Revision Act of 2006 has expanded the meaning of "famous marks". A mark, according to the Revision Act, is required to be

---

47 Brian Gearing, 'Moseley V. V Secret Catalogue, Inc.' (2004) 19 *Berkeley Technology Law Journal* <http://scholarship.law.berkeley.edu/cgi/viewcontent.cgi?article=1449&context=btlj> accessed 29 March 2015.

48 Michael A Epstein and Michael A Epstein, *Epstein On Intellectual Property* (Aspen Publishers 2006), 7-37.

49 *Hasbro, Inc v Clue Computing, Inc* [1999] 66 F Supp 2d (District Court Massachusetts).

50 Micheletti and Dorfman, 1350.

51 Ibid.

extensively recognized by the general consumers residing in the US, exclusive of marks that are only known in particular geographical spheres or niche markets.[52] The Revision Act also protects marks that are descriptive in nature but due to widespread use, have acquired uniqueness. If a mark has been registered, the degree of actual recognition of such, products or services sold under such mark and the publicity and advertisement of the mark are points to take into account to understand if the mark has attained the necessary degree of fame.[53] Moreover, irrespective of economic harm, likelihood of dilution-by-blurring has been made actionable expressly. The Revision Act defines dilution as an "association arising from the similarity between a mark or trade name and a famous mark that impairs the distinctiveness of the famous mark".[54] Simply the likelihood of dilution is needed to be shown for the purpose of obtaining relief as per the Revision Act.[55] Rather than choosing to wait till the occurrence of actual harm, the intention is to give trademark owners a way to stop dilution at the initial stage.

In considering a claim of blurring, the Revision Act mentions that courts are required to take into account numerous factors for the purpose of determining if dilution is likely to follow. This includes the similarity between the junior and the original mark, degree of inherent or attained uniqueness of the original mark, if usage of the well-known original mark is "substantially exclusive", the scope of recognition of such well known mark, intention of the junior user and "actual association" (if in existence) between the original and the junior mark.[56]

In light of the above, not having to require showing of "actual dilution" and specific recognition of dilution by blurring according to the Revision Act has certainly contributed in making the concept of blurring much easier to understand.

6. Confusing the Concept of Dilution by Blurring with Infringement

A claim of infringement, in simple words, may occur when a trademark is stolen from the original user by another, for the purpose of tempting

---

[52] Jeffrey Katz and David Weems, 'Almost Famous? Comments On The Trademark Dilution Revision Act' [2007] *The Metropolitan Corporate Counsel*.
[53] Ibid.
[54] The Trademark Dilution Revision Act of 2006 (TRDA).
[55] Ibid.
[56] Ibid.

consumers to purchase products or services of the junior user, therefore confusing it with the original user.[57] The idea of protection is so that consumers are confident that a product they wish to purchase contains the same unique features as when they purchased the same product in the past.[58] A likelihood of confusion test is applied by courts for the purpose of analyzing infringement claims. The chances that a significant amount of sensible regular consumers are likely to be confused or misled, considering the source of the concerned products, are measured through such tests.[59] Strength of the original mark, degree of resemblance among two marks, closeness of the goods, possibility that the original owner would channel the gap, actual confusion, good faith of the junior user in adopting its own mark, the quality of the junior user's product, and buyers' sophistication are certain factors the courts have developed in assessing consumer's likelihood of confusion.[60]

The dilution doctrine has been often misconstrued by courts as consequence of infringement.[61] For the purpose of sustaining a dilution claim, the requirement that confusion must be found has been the basis of such a misunderstanding. Previous decisions addressed dilution by blurring claims using infringement standards or decided such claims with the language of infringement. Courts seem to be relaxed with decisions made in acknowledgement of infringement standards that focus on the protection of the general public.[62] Courts, however, have always been uncomfortable in giving trademark owners a stronger weapon of remedy due to trademark dilution –fearing that such acknowledgement (especially in dilution-by-blurring) might give property rights in gross to mark owners, rather than the usual quasi-property right.[63]

In a case that involved the defendants trying to use the mark "Blockbuster" in fireworks, the Eighth Circuit quoted the following, which clearly describes the difference between blurring and infringement:

---

[57] Legal Information Institute, Cornell University Law School, 'Trademark Infringement' <https://www.law.cornell.edu/wex/trademark_infringement> accessed 16 April 2015.

[58] David Radack, 'Likelihood Of Confusion—The Basis For Trademark Infringement' (*The Minerals, Metals & Materials Society*, 2002) <http://www.tms.org/pubs/journals/jom/matters/matters-0212.html> accessed 16 April 2015.

[59] Mark Lemley and Stacey Dogan, 'Grounding Trademark Law Through Trademark Use' [2007] *Stanford Public Law Working Paper* 1670, 1674.

[60] Legal Information Institute, Cornell University Law School.

[61] R.S Nelson, 'Unraveling The Trademark Rope: Tarnishment And Its Proper Place In The Laws Of Unfair Competition' (2002) 42 *IDEA* 133, 135-136.

[62] McCabe, 1828.

[63] Paul Edward Kim, 'Preventing Dilution Of The Federal Trademark Dilution Act: Why The FTDA Requires Actual Economic Harm' (2001) 150 *University of Pennsylvania Law Review* 319, 337.

> If a parent says to the kids, 'Let's go pick something out at Blockbuster tonight,' and the youngest child assumes they will be buying fireworks made by Viacom, that is evidence of the confusion that is essential to a claim of trademark infringement. But if the oldest child answers, 'Which Blockbuster,' that evidences dilution by blurring.[64]

Even when consumer confusion would not be present, the courts' decisions that injunctive relief would still be provided has basically established the concept of a dilution claim. Although both infringement and dilution may be in existence together at a particular circumstance, courts have recognized both as separate claims. The First Circuit in *Esquire, Inc. v. Esquire Slipper Manufacturing Co., Inc.* stated that in spite of there being no presence of consumer confusion, addressing the dilution matter as a separate claim was a relief. Upholding a state anti-dilution statute, the Seventh Circuit in the case *Polaroid Corp. v. Polaroid, Inc.* quoted that dilution injury "differs materially from that arising out of the orthodox confusion" and "such confusion leads to immediate injury, while dilution is an infection which, if allowed to spread, will inevitably destroy the advertising value of the mark".[65]

The other side has unfortunately persisted more. By the year 1996, it is notable that sixteen cases were decided on dilution standards, while most dilution matters were decided by taking into account the traditional infringement standards.[66] For instance, the New York state court in *Cue Publishing Co., Inc. v. Colgate-Palmolive Co.* stated that the presence of some measure of confusion is required for the effective dilution doctrine.[67] Confusion is required to be portrayed in accordance to New York State's anti-dilution law, as mentioned by a federal court in New York in the case of *Geisel v. Poynter Products, InC.*[68] Moreover, although the Fifth Circuit agreed that dilution may occur at circumstances where no likelihood of confusion exists, the court stated that since marks of the two cases, namely *Publishing Co., Inc. v. Colgate-Palmolive Co.* and New York in the case of *Geisel v. Poynter Products, InC.,* were not "confusing", dilution in this case was

---

[64] McCabe, 1829.

[65] Bruce E. Altschuler and Celia A. Sgroi, *Understanding Law In A Changing Society* (Prentice Hall 1996), 203.

[66] Stacey Dogan and Mark Lemley, 'The Trademark Use Requirement In Dilution Cases' (2007) 24 *Santa Clara Computer & High Technology Law Journal* 541, 548.

[67] *Cue Publishing Company v Colgate-Palmolive Co* [1964] 233 F. Supp. 443 (S.D.N.Y. 1964).

[68] *Geisel v Poynter Products Inc* [1968] 283 F. Supp. 261 (S.D.N.Y. 1968).

inappropriate according to the Fifth Circuit.[69] This was widely criticized by scholars, due to the courts' determination of dilution using infringement standards. However, the term confusion actually meant "dissimilarity", according to the concerned court. Notably, "confusion" has already become a term associated precisely with findings of infringement over the years and thus courts' use of such may be misleading towards the audience, while lessening the precision of courts' reasoning.[70] Such inappropriate language can lead to the misapplication of the dilution rule.

Factors such as resemblance of the goods, sophistication of customers, predatory intention and renown of the junior mark are universal factors also used in determining likelihood of confusion.[71] The *Mead Data Central* factors however, irrespective of their shortcomings, encouraged courts to analyze dilution-by-blurring as a separate claim. Furthermore, although the Federal Dilution Act contained "likelihood of confusion" by adopting dilution's common law definition, the drafters' intent was made clear. The House Report stated that,

> …dilution does not rely upon the standard test of infringement, that is, likelihood of confusion, deception or mistake. Rather, it applies when the unauthorized use of a famous mark reduces the public's perception that the mark signifies something unique, singular, or particular.[72]

It is important to note that even after the enactment of the Act, courts have continued to struggle with the idea of dilution, different from infringement, not needing a presentation of consumer confusion. Due to the availability of previous case law examining infringement claims, perhaps it makes it easier for courts to examine a violation of dilution under such standards.

---

[69] Ibid.

[70] Mark Partridge, 'Understanding Trademark Law's Key Principle' (*Pattishall McAuliffe*) <http://www.pattishall.com/pdf/LikelihoodofConfusion.pdf> accessed 19 April 2015.

[71] Eugene Quinn, 'Trademark Infringement—The Likelihood Of Confusion' (*Sans technology Institute*, 2008) <http://www.sans.edu/research/leadership-laboratory/article/quinn-ip-confusion> accessed 19 April 2015.

[72] 112th Congress, House Report, 'THE FEDERAL TRADEMARK DILUTION ACT (`FTDA')' (2012) <http://thomas.loc.gov/cgi-bin/cpquery/?&sid=cp112MHseG&r_n=hr647.112&dbname=cp112&&sel=TOC_2861&> accessed 19 April 2015.

7. IN QUEST OF A SOLUTION

The optional factors for the purpose of assessing likelihood of blurring provide a relatively straightforward roadmap to the courts, in comparison to the *Nabisco* test containing ten factors. It is also worth mentioning that the list excludes competition and consumer confusion, factors which aided the conflict between infringement and dilution. Increased guidance is provided to the courts with regards to dilution by blurring, setting a "likelihood of dilution" standard as a requirement for a remedy.[73] With an exception of the following areas, where attention may be given, dilution by blurring has been well addressed by the Act, thus eliminating the confusion with infringement.

The factor of "extent to which the owner of the famous mark is engaging in substantially exclusive use of the mark",[74] mentioned in the Revision Act, may be problematic since it may limit the Revision Act shielding marks with acquired distinctiveness.[75] Moreover, since for instance United Airlines would fail to establish a considerably exclusive usage of the "United" trademark, in accordance with the Revision Act, it would not seem probable to prevail on a dilution by blurring claim for the mark "United" – thus limiting acquired distinctiveness.[76] Lastly, the factors may fail to provide courts with satisfactory guidance when considering whether association between marks is likely to harm the famous mark's uniqueness. McCarthy's suggestions may be taken into account.[77] He mentions that courts must necessitate evidence or expert testimony for the purpose of establishing the impairment portion.[78]

8. CONCLUSION

It is evident that dilution-by-blurring has become overtime a conceptually difficult area of trademark law, considering that it was misunderstood (also chosen at instances) by courts as trademark infringement. Moreover, even upon being able to view it as a separate claim, courts were broadly split in

---

[73] Jennifer Beerline, 'Anti-Dilution Law, New And Improved: The Trademark Dilution Revision Act Of 2006' (2008) 23 *Berkeley Technology Law Journal* 511, 531.
[74] TRDA.
[75] Ibid.
[76] Paul Heald and Robert Brauneis, 'Trademark Infringement, Trademark Dilution, And The Decline In Sharing Of Famous Brand Names: An Introduction And Empirical Study' [2010] University of Georgia Law, Research Paper Series <http://digitalcommons.law.uga.edu/cgi/viewcontent.cgi?article=1071&context=fac_wp> accessed 19 April 2015.
[77] McCarthy.
[78] Gregory J Battersby and Charles W Grimes, *Licensing Royalty Rates* (Aspen Publishers 2005), 236.

two, while variations in court decisions are well observed. No doubt revision made by the Trademark Dilution Revision Act 2006 has contributed in the better understanding of blurring; however, taking care of the aforementioned areas would further conceptualize dilution by blurring.

Works Cited

Primary Sources

Legislation

The Federal Trademark Dilution Act, 1995.
The Trademark Dilution Revision Act, 2006.

Case Law

Cue Publishing Company v Colgate-Palmolive Co [1964] 233 F. Supp. 443 (S.D.N.Y. 1964).

Geisel v Poynter Products Inc [1968] 283 F. Supp. 261 (S.D.N.Y. 1968).

Hasbro, Inc v Clue Computing, Inc [1999] 66 F Supp 2d (District Court Massachusetts) 117.

Mead Data Central v Toyota Motor Sales [1988] 702 F Supp (District Court Southern District of New York) 1031.

Panavision Int'l, LP v Toeppen [1998] 141 F3d (9th Circuit) 1316.

Perfumebaycom Inc v eBay, Inc [2007] 506 F3d (9th Circuit) 1165.

Sally Gee, Inc v Myra Hogan, Inc [1983] 699 F2d (2nd Circuit) 621.

Times Mirror Magazines, Inc v Las Vegas Sports News, LLC [2000] 212 F3d (3rd Circuit) 157.

Westchester Media Co, LP v PRL USA Holdings, Inc [2000] 214 F3d (5th Circuit).

Zinn v Seruga [2009] Civ No 05-3572 (District Court New York).

Secondary Sources

Books

Epstein M and Epstein M, *Epstein On Intellectual Property* (Aspen Publishers 2006).

Ferrera G, *Cyberlaw* (South-Western Cengage Learning 2012).

Handelman H, *Guide To Trademark Trial And Appeal Board Practice* (Aspen Publishers Online 2007).

Sakulin W, *Trademark Protection And Freedom Of Expression* (Kluwer Law International 2011).

Articles and Essays

Beebe B, 'A Defense of the New Federal Trademark Antidilution Law' (2006) 16 Fordham Intellectual Property, Media and Entertainment Law Journal 1142.

Beerline J, 'Anti-Dilution Law, New And Improved: The Trademark Dilution Revision Act Of 2006' (2008) 23 Berkeley Technology Law Journal 511.

Bunker M and Bissell K, 'Lost In The Semiotic Maze: Empirical Approaches To Proof Of Blurring In Trademark Dilution Law' (2013) 18 Communication Law and Policy 375.

Burgunder L, 'Trademark Protection Of Smells: Sense Or Nonsense' (1991) 29 Am Business Law Journal 459.

Gearing B, 'Moseley v. V Secret Catalogue, Inc.' (2004) 19 Berkeley Technology Law Journal 221.

Gray M, 'Defending Against A Dilution Claim: A Practitioner's Guide' (1996) 205 Texas Intellectual Property Law Journal 206.

Holt K and Duvall S, 'Chasing Moseley's Ghost: Dilution Surveys Under The Trademark Dilution Revision Act' (2008) 98 The Law Journal of the International Trademark Association 1311.

Ilanah S, 'The Actual Dilution Requirement In The United States, United Kingdom And European Union: A Comparative Analysis' (2006) 12 Boston University Journal of Science and Technology Law 271.

Katz J and Weems D, 'Almost Famous? Comments On The Trademark Dilution Revision Act' [2007] The Metropolitan Corporate Counsel.

Kim P, 'Preventing Dilution Of The Federal Trademark Dilution Act: Why The FTDA Requires Actual Economic Harm' (2001) 150 University of Pennsylvania Law Review 319.

Lemley M and Dogan S, 'Grounding Trademark Law Through Trademark Use' [2007] Stanford Public Law Working Paper 1670.

Londesborough S, 'Should Colours Be Protected By Trade Mark Law? What Problems May Arise In Protecting Them?' (Undergraduate, University of Kent).

Marans J, '*Westchester Media Co. L.P., et al. v. PRL USA Holdings, Inc.*: The Fight Over The Name, POLO' (2002) 8 Jeffrey S. Moorad Sports Law Journal 351.

McCabe K, 'Dilution-By-Blurring: A Theory Caught In the Shadow of Trademark Infringement' (1999) 68 Fordham Law Review 1827.

Micheletti C and Dorfman D, 'Proving Dilution By Blurring: An Analysis Of Dilution By Blurring Factors Under The Federal Trademark Dilution Act' (2002) 92 Official Journal of the International Trademark Association 1345.

Mermin J, 'Interpreting The Federal Trademark Dilution Act Of 1995: The Logic Of The Actual Dilution Requirement' (2001) 42 Boston College Law Review 207.

Nelson R, 'Unraveling The Trademark Rope: Tarnishment And Its Proper Place In The Laws Of Unfair Competition' (2002) 42 IDEA 133.

Oswald L, '"Tarnishment" And "Blurring" Under The Federal Trademark Dilution Act Of 1995' (1999) 36 American Business Law Journal 255.

Olson A, 'Dilution by Tarnishment: An Unworkable Cause of Action in Cases Of Artistic Expression' (2012) 53 Boston College Law Review 693.

Schechter F, 'The Rational Basis Of Trademark Protection' (1927) 40 Harvard Law Review 813.

Terry A and Chittock C, 'Shapes And Slogans As Trade Marks: Developments In Case Law.' (2010) 18 Journal of Brand Management 174.

Vadim V, 'Moseley V. Secret Catalogue, Inc.: Redefining The Scope Of The Federal Trademark Dilution Act' (2012) 77 St. John's Law Review 675.

Voss M, 'Ringling Bros.-Barnum & Bailey Combined Shows, Inc. V. Utah Division Of Travel Development & Nabisco, Inc. V. PF Brands, Inc.' (2000) 15 Berkeley Technology Law Journal 265.

Internet Sources

Leach S, 'The Federal Trademark Dilution Act Of 1995 Has Not Brought Uniformity And Consistency To The Protection Of Famous Marks' (Snell & Wilmer, 2002) <http://www.swlaw.com/assets/pdf/publications/2002/11/09/Trademark-Dilution-by-Sid-Leach.pdf> accessed 28 March 2015.

Legal Information Institute, Cornell University Law School, 'Trademark Infringement' <https://www.law.cornell.edu/wex/trademark_infringement> accessed 16 April 2015.

Radack D, 'Likelihood of Confusion – The Basis for Trademark Infringement' (The Minerals, Metals & Materials Society, 2002) <http://www.tms.org/pubs/journals/jom/matters/matters-0212.html> accessed 16 April 2015.

Saner E, 'You Can't Trademark Everything' (*The Guardian*, 2013) <http://www.theguardian.com/law/shortcuts/2013/jun/04/you-cant-trademark-everything-chanel> accessed 16 April 2015.

Sweeney D, 'Can You Trademark A Sound?' *The Huffington Post* (2014) <http://www.huffingtonpost.com/deborah-sweeney/can-you-trademark-a-sound_b_5635571.html> accessed 16 April 2015.

World Intellectual Property Organization (WIPO), 'About Trademarks' (2015) <http://www.wipo.int/trademarks/en/about_trademarks.html#function> accessed 25 March 2015.

Case Comment
Haile v London Borough of Waltham Forest [2015]

Christopher Busst[†]

A homeless person may be owed a duty to be re-housed by a local housing authority if they can meet the requirements set out in the Housing Act 1996. The authority does not owe the full duty, however, in circumstances where the homeless person has made themselves 'intentionally homeless' - where they have carried out a deliberate act or omission which has led to their loss of accommodation. The House of Lords ruling in Din v Wandsworth London Borough Council *[1983]*[1] *had created a consistent and certain approach to findings of intentionality. The Supreme Court in* Haile[2] *claims not to have departed from the reasoning in* Din. *Still, it will be shown that the express findings in* Haile *have completely changed the approach to intentionality. Despite the Supreme Court's protestations to the contrary, a certain deliberate act by a homeless person can now be ignored if, hypothetically, the homeless person would have become homeless anyway—creating a causational nightmare for authority decision makers.*

Keywords: Housing Act 1996; Intentional homelessness; *Din*; *Haile*.

---

† Senior Lecturer, University of Wolverhampton Law School.

[1] *Din v Wandsworth London Borough Council* [1983] 1 AC 657.

[2] *Haile v London Borough of Waltham Forest* [2015] UKSC 34, [2015] AC 1471.

1. BACKGROUND LAW

The Housing Act 1996, Part VII, governs the duties owed by a housing authority to the homeless. S.193 contains the 'full housing duty', requiring that the housing authority shall 'secure that accommodation is available for occupation by the applicant', in circumstances where:

> (1) .... the local housing authority are satisfied that an applicant is homeless, eligible for assistance and has a priority need, and are not satisfied that he became homeless intentionally.

Intentionality is defined at s.191:

> (1) A person becomes homeless intentionally if he deliberately does or fails to do anything in consequence of which he ceases to occupy accommodation which is available for his occupation and which it would have been reasonable for him to continue to occupy.

Much of the relevant case law was decided before the Housing Act 1996 came into force. Its predecessor, however, the Housing (Homeless Persons) Act 1977, contained an almost identical provision at section 17.

2. FACTUAL BACKGROUND TO *HAILE*

The appellant was the tenant of a bed-sitting room in a hostel in Leyton, London. On 25th October 2011, she surrendered the bed-sitting room of her own accord, because she was unhappy about smells in the hostel.

She moved into temporary accommodation in Kings Cross until November 2011, when she had to leave due to over-crowding. On 24th November 2011, she applied as homeless to London Borough of Waltham Forest ('the Authority'). The Authority provided her with temporary accommodation, where she remained until the date of the Supreme Court decision.

On 15th February 2012, she gave birth to her daughter. It was accepted that the terms of the appellant's original tenancy in Leyton were such that she would have had to leave the accommodation once her child was born. On 1st August 2012, the Authority decided that although homeless, eligible and in priority need, she was also intentionally homeless. Applying s.191 of the Housing Act 1996, she had given up accommodation in Leyton in October

2011 that was (at the time she left) available for her and reasonable for her continued occupation. The fact that she had given birth was deemed irrelevant, as it was not 'in consequence' of her daughter's birth that she had lost the Leyton accommodation.

The Authority upheld its decision on review in January 2013. This review decision fell to be considered on appeal by the Supreme Court.

3. The Decision in *Haile*

The issue for the Supreme Court was whether the birth of the baby broke the chain of causation for intentionality, as the applicant would have been homeless anyway by the time the application was considered. The Supreme Court held that it did, ruled that the Authority's decision was erroneous and overturned the finding of intentionality.

Lord Reed, giving the lead judgment, stated that the review officer's decision was deficient because 'no consideration was given to the question whether the cause of her current state of homelessness was her surrender of the tenancy of the room in the hostel'.[3] If that question had been asked, then the only reasonable conclusion would be, 'no it had not'.

Much of Lord Reed's judgment relied on the earlier case of *Dyson.*[4] He uses this as authority for the proposal that a two-stage process is required when deciding a question of intentionality. First, applying s.191,[5] a housing authority must decide if the person had ceased to occupy accommodation due to a deliberate act or omission. Second, s.193[6] required an authority to consider if the current homelessness was the result of that deliberate act, or a different event.[7]

Lord Reed describes this as a 'but for' test of causation[8] and concludes that, due to the birth of the baby, it could not be said that 'if she had not done that deliberate act she would not have become homeless'.[9] Therefore, she would still have been homeless at the time of her homeless application, even if she had remained in her Leyton accommodation. In explaining his reasoning Lord Reed gives the example of an elderly man becoming homeless when his care home closes and then being found intentionally homeless due to his being

[3] Ibid.
[4] *Dyson v Kerrier District Council* [1980] 1 WLR 1205 CA.
[5] Housing Act 1996.
[6] Housing Act 1996.
[7] *Haile*, para 26–27.
[8] *Haile*, para 30.
[9] *Haile*, para 67.

evicted from 'student digs' as a young man because of rowdy parties. He finds this absurd as there is no causal connection between the current homelessness and the historic eviction.[10]

Lord Reed also focuses on public policy. He decides, without full explanation, that 'the policy underlying the provisions as to intentional homelessness' is 'to prevent queue-jumping'.[11] This finding leads him to conclude that the applicant was not queue-jumping and so his decision must therefore be consistent with the public policy of the legislation.

Most interestingly, the Supreme Court goes to great lengths to find that the decision being made is consistent with the existing authority on intentionality. Prior to *Haile,* the key authority for intentional homelessness was *Din*[12]—which had been relied on by practitioners and housing authorities for over 30 years. Lord Reed in his judgment states of *Din* that the decision 'appears to me to have been correct and to remain good law'.[13]

Lord Neuberger, in *Haile*, stresses that the Supreme Court should be 'very slow before departing from an earlier decision of this court or the House of Lords'.[14] He cites *Fitzleet*[15] as authority that precedent should not be departed from even perhaps if an earlier decision is wrong, as it provides certainty and an orderly development of the rules. He also cites, with approval, a recent judgment of Lord Hodge who stated:

> Where Parliament re-enacts a statutory provision, which has been the subject of authoritative judicial interpretation, the court will readily infer that Parliament intended the re-enacted provision to bear the meaning that case law had already established.[16]

The relevant provisions in the Housing Act 1996, as we have seen, were a direct re-enactment of the Housing (Homeless Persons) Act 1977. Lord Neuberger accepted therefore that 'if this appeal could not be allowed without departing from *Din*, it should be dismissed'.[17] He was convinced, with some 'hesitation' however, that Lord Reed's argument did not 'involve departing

---

[10] *Haile*, para 28–29.
[11] *Haile*, para 67.
[12] *Din v Wandsworth London Borough Council* [1983] 1 AC 657 (HL).
[13] *Haile*, para 9.
[14] *Haile*, para 73.
[15] *Fitzleet Estates Ltd v Cherry (Inspector of Taxes)* [1977] 1 WLR 1345 (HL).
[16] *R (on the applications of ZH and CN) v London Borough of Newham and London Borough of Lewisham* [2014] UKSC 62, [2014] 3 WLR 1548 53.
[17] *Haile*, para 72.

from the reasoning of the majority in *Din*'.[18] It is therefore worthwhile setting out briefly the facts of *Din* to examine this claim.

4. FACTUAL BACKGROUND TO *DIN*

The applicants in *Din* rented a flat in Wandsworth and had fallen into considerable rent arrears due to the failure of their business. There was no suggestion that they had any fault in the build-up of arrears, but in their reduced financial circumstances they simply could not afford to pay the rent. The family approached the local housing authority and were advised to remain in the flat until evicted.

The applicant was served with a distress warrant in August 1979 and he and his family abandoned the Wandsworth flat and move into unsuitable temporary accommodation until December 1979. At this point they were required to leave the temporary accommodation and applied to the relevant authority as homeless. It was accepted by all parties that by December 1979 the family would have been evicted from the Wandsworth flat and become homeless anyway.

5. THE DECISION IN *DIN*

The applicant in *Din* was found to be intentionally homeless. He had carried out a deliberate act in leaving accommodation available for him (the Wandsworth flat). This was the operative cause of his homelessness, it did not matter that he would have lost the accommodation by the time of his homeless application.[19]

6. DOES THE JUDGMENT IN *HAILE* INVOLVE DEPARTING WITH THE REASONING IN DIN?

The key departure in *Haile* from the findings in *Din* revolves around whether or not a hypothetical rather than an actual cause of homelessness can be used to absolve an applicant of the stigma of intentionality.

---

[18] *Haile*, para 79.
[19] *Din* (HL).

It is noteworthy that counsel for the unsuccessful appellant in *Din* raised almost identical arguments to those espoused by Lord Reed in *Haile*. Counsel contended that there 'must be an unbroken chain of causation but the chain was broken by the fact that...the tenancy would in any event have been terminated by December', and that 'it is always the homelessness of the applicant at the time of the application that is being enquired into'.[20]

This argument was given short shrift by the majority in *Din*. Lord Wilberforce, handing down the lead judgment, confirmed that although it was argued that the applicant would have been homeless anyway, that the original cause of homelessness had ceased to operate and that there must be a causal nexus between the original act and the homelessness subsisting at the time of the decision, he was 'unable to accept this argument'. Such an argument 'cannot be reconciled with the wording of the Act' which 'is completely and repeatedly clear in concentrating attention on when the appellants became homeless, and requiring the question of intention to be ascertained as at that time'.[21] An authority could not be required to look into hypotheses, what might have happened had the appellants not moved, and such a finding would add 'greatly to the difficulties of the local authority's task in administering this Act'.[22]

In *Din*, Lord Fraser agreed that hypothetical reasons for homelessness could not be relied on 'if he actually became homeless deliberately, the fact that he might, or would, have been homeless for other reasons at the date of the inquiry is irrelevant'.[23]

Lord Carnwath dissented in *Haile,* as he felt that Lord Reed's reasoning was not consistent with that in *Din*; which he cited with approval.[24] He considered that the law had been consistent for over 20 years, and that the wording of the relevant provisions had not changed with the introduction of the Housing Act 1996. Lord Reed had undertaken 'his own re-analysis of *Din* in a way not suggested by the parties before us, nor (to my knowledge) by anyone else in the three decades since it was decided'.[25] This re-analysis was not desirable or necessary. The review officer's decision was 'a perfectly orthodox reflection of the majority approach in *Din*'.[26] The appeal should fail quite simply because 'the birth of her child might have been, but was not, the

[20] *Din* (HL), 658.
[21] *Din* (HL), 667.
[22] *Din* (HL), 667.
[23] *Din* (HL), 672.
[24] *Haile*, para 89.
[25] Ibid.
[26] Ibid.

actual cause of her loss of either the original or the temporary accommodation'.[27]

Lord Reed, in *Haile,* appears to justify his re-interpretation in part, by explaining that the law has changed in two ways since *Din*. He refers to Lord Lowry's judgment in *Din* as making reference to the causal link being described 'in terms of continuing homelessness' and that this condition continued until the appellant obtained 'non-temporary or "settled" accommodation'.[28] He claimed that this concept had been overturned by the case of *Awua*[29] where events other than the obtaining of settled accommodation were held to break the chain of causation and 'confirmed that the necessary connection between the deliberate conduct required by the definition of "becoming homeless intentionally" and the applicant's homelessness at the time of the enquiry was causal'.[30]

The concept of 'settled' accommodation described in *Din* was, however, expressly approved in *Awua* but further defined. Lord Hoffman held that the occupation of settled accommodation (something more than temporary accommodation) as an act that might break the chain of causation for intentionality was 'well established...and nothing I have said is intended to cast any doubt upon it'.[31] Nevertheless, Lord Hoffman continued to state that this was only one of the potential acts that might break the chain, although he in fact reserved judgment on whether it was the 'sole and exclusive method' for doing so, as this point had been conceded by the housing authority in that case.[32]

In *Din*, only Lord Lowry had made reference to a need for homelessness to be continuous and Lord Hoffman answered this point, confirming that 'what persists until the causal link is broken is the intentionality, not the homelessness'.[33]

These points help little in re-aligning *Haile* and *Din*. Lord Hoffman, in *Awua,* maintained that hypothetical causes could not be relied on to break the chain of causation. He cited Lord Fraser in *Din* with approval and maintained that an 'argument, based on what would have hypothetically happened had she

[27] *Haile*, para 93.
[28] *Haile*, para 11.
[29] *R v Brent London Borough Council, Ex p Awua* [1996] AC 55.
[30] *Haile*, para 11.
[31] *Awua*, 69.
[32] Ibid.
[33] Ibid.

have done something different, is precluded by the decision of this House in *Din*'.[34]

Since *Awua,* a variety of cases have relied on events other than the obtaining of settled accommodation to break the chain of causation. In *Fahia,*[35] the loss of temporary accommodation due to a significant reduction in Housing Benefit, that made the accommodation unaffordable, broke the chain of causation. In *Bassett,*[36] the House of Lords found that an applicant leaving settled accommodation to move to Canada with her husband was not intentionally homeless. On the couple's return to England they lived with the husband's sister, however, the couple split and the applicant was required to leave her sister in law's home. It was the breakdown of her marriage that led to the loss of her accommodation and broke the chain of causation, not the move to Canada.

Similarly, the Court of Appeal in *Aranda*[37] considered the applicant was not intentionally homeless when she left settled accommodation in England to move to Colombia with little capital and no job. The chain of causation was broken by the breakdown of her relationship, which led to the loss of her Colombian accommodation, Henry L.J. finding that 'the husband's abandonment of his family broke the chain of causation between her decision to surrender the Camden tenancy…and her eventual homelessness, thereby making it impossible to find intentional homelessness as a result of that choice'.[38]

Every relevant case before *Haile* required an event to have actually occurred that intervened to prevent the intentionality from being operative. Lord Carnwath, in his dissenting speech in *Haile* summarised the position perfectly, all these cases show is that to break the chain of causation, the

> …intervening accommodation comes to an end due to a change of circumstances for reasons not directly linked to its temporary nature....the key to these cases is that the new event is the direct cause of the eventual homelessness, and is treated as its operative cause, thus breaking the chain of causation from the (intentional) loss of the previous settled accommodation.[39]

---

[34] *Awua*, 73.
[35] *R v Harrow London Council, Ex p Fahia* [1996] 29 HLR 94 (HL).
[36] *R v Basingstoke and Deane Borough Council, Ex p Bassett* [1983] 10 HLR 125.
[37] *R v Camden London Borough Council, Ex p Aranda* [1998] 30 H.L.R. 76.
[38] Ibid., 88.
[39] *Haile*, para 92.

The lack of consistency in the Supreme Court's approach in *Haile* can be demonstrated by returning to Lord Reed's simplistic example of the elderly man being evicted from a closing care home. Following the principles in *Din,* an authority should look for an actual event taking place that caused his homelessness. In this case, the closure of the care home would seem to be the operative cause of his (clearly unintentional) homelessness.

Imagine the same elderly man however reading for his degree as a mature student. He is a violent man and is evicted from his student digs for severe nuisance and for assaulting a fellow student in the May of his final year of study. He sleeps rough until the end of his undergraduate studies in June (when he would have had to leave his digs anyway) and presents as homeless in July to the relevant authority.

Following *Din,* the deliberate act causing his homelessness (the violence and nuisance) means that he is intentionally homeless. Following Lord Reed's analysis in *Haile,* however he is not intentionally homeless: the assault causing his eviction is ignored and an event that did not cause his homelessness (the end of the University year) is the operative event, a complete departure from the earlier case law.

What of the public policy issue raised by Lord Reed in *Haile?* This is also expressly dismissed as a key factor in *Din*. Lord Lowry found that the applicants in *Din* were equally free of blame—stating that 'there is, to my mind, no question here of queue-jumping or other unmeritorious conduct'.[40] Despite this, the public policy consideration could not overcome his 'applying the law...to the facts' and therefore holding that 'the appellants lost their priority by becoming homeless in a relevant way'.[41]

7. THE IMPACT OF *HAILE*

The Supreme Court, in *Haile,* felt compassion for the applicant, yet could not easily distinguish *Din* and *Awua*. Attempting to do so, Lord Reed pointed to an actual event in *Haile* (the birth of the daughter), that would have led to the appellant becoming homeless anyway by the time of the homeless application, whereas in *Din* there was merely a possibility that they might have been evicted. Even Lord Neuberger in his consenting speech accepted that this 'is a rather narrow ground for distinguishing the earlier decision in *Din*'.[42]

---

[40] *Din* (HL), 681.
[41] Ibid.
[42] *Haile*, para 80.

After an examination of the previous authority, especially the cases of *Din* and *Awua,* it can be seen that the reasoning of the majority in both cases has not been followed. Events that might have hypothetically led to a loss of accommodation are being used to justify a break in the chain of causation rather than the actual reason for the loss (something that the earlier cases were keen to avoid). Had the Supreme Court in *Haile* accepted that it was departing from the reasoning of the majority in *Din* and set out new causational guidelines for local housing authority decision makers, then this would have at least allowed some certainty. Instead, it has left a review officer to second-guess when a court might decide that an event had broken the chain of causation.

The potential effect of the judgment in *Haile* is far reaching. Authorities can no longer look to the actual cause of the applicant's homelessness but need to consider also any number of hypothetical eventualities that might have had the same effect. Even more unsatisfactory is that over twenty years of certainty has been disturbed by the Supreme Court, leaving two seemingly contradictory decisions both of which are still maintained to be 'good' law.

Case Comment: Recent Developments in the Extraterritorial Scope of Application of the ECHR in the Aftermath of *Jaloud v The Netherlands* [2014]

Stefanos Xenofontos†

In an age of globalization, as a result of the ongoing global 'war on terror,' and the rise in foreign military interventions, states' military conduct is increasingly expanding outside their territorial boundaries. This phenomenon has caused an additional vulnerability for individuals, increasingly posing a threat to their human rights, and the right to life in particular, even across borders. This case comment examines the recent developments in the extraterritorial scope of application of the European Convention on Human Rights (ECHR) as they arise from the recent judgment in Jaloud v The Netherlands *(2014).*[1] *Particular emphasis will be given to the legal difficulties in protecting the human right to life, in the context of multinational military operations overseas; as well as the developing trend towards further extending a state's scope of jurisdiction in foreign battlefields. As the jurisprudence of the UK national courts indicates, Jaloud's new 'checkpoint' test for jurisdiction, leaves the door wide-open for establishing the ECHR States' jurisdiction in*

---

† LLM Public International Law, University of Leicester; Secretary-General, European Law Students' Association UK.

[1] *Jaloud v The Netherlands* [GC], no. 47708/08, § 142, ECHR 20 November 2014.

aerial bombardments (previously rejected in Bankovic[2]*), or targeted killings by drones in the context of future operations. Certainly, such a finding would open the way for the courts to challenge governmental decisions on major policy choices in foreign affairs and further judicialise armed forces' conduct.*

Keywords: Human Rights, Extraterritoriality, Jurisdiction, Armed Conflict, Military Operations, Drones.

1. INTRODUCTION

Adding to the growing jurisprudence of the European Court of Human Rights (ECtHR), concerning the extraterritorial application of the Convention, and the protection of the right to life—in the context of military operations overseas—*Jaloud* introduced some interesting jurisdictional and practical aspects on the issue. The case arose out of the fatal shooting of Jaloud by Dutch troops, while the car in which he was a passenger attempted to pass through a checkpoint in south-eastern Iraq without stopping for control.[3] The applicant argued that 'the respondent State had failed to meet its obligations to properly investigate the death of his son, with a view to bringing the person responsible to justice'.[4] Consequently, the Court was preliminarily concerned with establishing the necessary jurisdictional link between the respondent State, and the individual concerned, for the purposes of Article 1 ECHR; and also in order to engage the extra-territorial application of the European Convention on Human Rights. Subsequently, the ECtHR in assessing the case on its merits examined the alleged violation of the state's procedural obligations under Article 2 ECHR. For the purposes of the present case comment, emphasis will be given to the legal challenges with applying human right to life (as codified in Article 2 ECHR), in the context of armed conflict and multinational military operations abroad, as these arise from the *Jaloud* judgment. The possible effects of the case on the extra-territoriality of the

---

2 *Bankovic and Others v Belgium and 16 Other Contracting States* [GC], no. 52207/99 (2001) 11 BHRC 435, [2001] ECHR 890.
3 Ibid., para 10–14.
4 Ibid., para 157.

ECHR will be discussed, as these are already demonstrated through the jurisprudence of national courts.

2. JURISDICTIONAL ISSUES ARISING FROM *JALOUD*

As scholarly literature suggests, jurisdiction and state responsibility, although inter-related, are two conceptually separate principles.[5] The relationship between the two raised new concerns in the wake of the judgment in *Jaloud,* concerning multinational military operations abroad.[6] Particular difficulties in establishing the Netherlands' jurisdiction, in this case, were posed by the fact that the incident took place in an area where the UK was an occupying power, and the Dutch troops were operating under the command of the British Armed Forces.[7] As indicated in this case, attribution of responsibility to the troop-contributing state can be a decisive factor in bringing the individual concerned under its jurisdiction for the purposes of Article 1 ECHR. The Court rejected the argument that Jaloud's death did not occur within the Netherlands' jurisdiction, because their troops were placed at the disposal of another state, holding the status of the UK as an 'occupying power' was not determinative in establishing the jurisdiction of the latter.[8] In retaining 'full command' over its military personnel and providing security in its area of operation, to the exclusion of other participating states, the Netherlands could not be 'divested of its "jurisdiction"' under the ECHR.[9] Particularly, the checkpoint where Jaloud was shot had been manned by Dutch soldiers under the command of a Dutch officer. This reasoning marked a significant departure from previous case law; demonstrating that just because Netherlands' troops formed part of a multinational force in pursuit of an international mandate, their conduct did not fall outside the scope of Article 1 ECHR.[10]

The Court then examined whether opening fire, against a person passing through a checkpoint, was sufficient to establish the necessary jurisdictional link between the respondent state and the applicant. In fact, this question

[5] Dominic McGoldrick, 'Extraterritorial Application of the International Covenant on Civil and Political Rights' in Coomans and Kamminga (eds), *Extraterritorial Application of Human Rights Treaties* (Intersentia 2004) 42-43; Marko Milanovic, *Extraterritorial Application of Human Rights Treaties: Law, Principles, and Policy* (OUP 2011) 41-53. See also *Jaloud*, 154.
[6] See eg, Jane Rooney, 'The Relationship between Jurisdiction and Attribution after *Jaloud v Netherlands*' (2015) 62 Neth Int Law Rev 407.
[7] See UNSC Res 1483 (22 May 2003) UN Doc S/RES/1483.
[8] *Jaloud*, para 142, 151.
[9] Ibid., para 143, 146, 149.
[10] Cf *Behrami v. France* (Admissibility Decision) (2007) 45 EHRR SE10, 70-71, 138-140, 149.

poses significant legal difficulties in protecting the right to life under these circumstances. The Court was required to consider *Bankovic* (since it has not been repealed) and thus clarified anew that the mere power to kill does not bring the target within the jurisdiction of the relevant state.[11] Before the *Jaloud* case arose, the ECtHR had only recognised two principles of extraterritorial jurisdiction: the personal and spatial; both of which are considered exceptions to the assumption, that jurisdictional competence of a state is primarily territorial.[12]

Importantly, the Dutch troops had not, at any time, exercised physical control over Jaloud by taking him into custody, thus rendering the application of personal jurisdiction unlikely. Additionally, the Court could not establish the Netherlands' jurisdiction based on the 'spatial model', used in *Al-Skeini*; since effective control over the relevant territory was exercised by the occupying power (i.e. the UK). The Netherlands' control of a checkpoint—temporary in nature and limited in space—could not be equated with exercising effective overall control over a territory. Instead, the necessary jurisdictional link was unanimously established by introducing a new test—on the basis that the Netherlands was exercising authority and control over 'persons passing through a checkpoint'.[13] Arguably, this hybrid 'checkpoint jurisdiction' is regarded as an expansion of the personal model of jurisdiction, because the Netherlands exercised full control and authority over its checkpoint and a logical build-up of territorial control due to the Netherlands' contribution of troops to the multinational operation during the occupation period.[14]

In following the purpose of the Convention, the ECHR demonstrated its willingness to extend the extraterritorial application of the Convention, and ensure effective protection of its fundamental rights abroad; thus overcoming some previous legal difficulties in securing the right to life in armed conflict situations. Noteworthy, the Court in *Jaloud* was not influenced by international policy considerations, to limit the extraterritoriality of the ECHR, as it had allegedly been in *Bankovic.*[15] Further, the ECHR was not prevented from establishing the requisite jurisdictional link, between the

[11] *Bankovic and Others v. Belgium and 16 Other Contracting States,* Decision of 1 Dec 2001, (2007) 44 EHRR SE5, 75.
[12] Ibid., para 57, 59-61, 67. See also, *Al-Skeini v. United Kingdom* (2011) 53 EHRR para 18, 132, 133-139.
[13] *Jaloud*, para 152.
[14] Ibid. See also, Friederycke Haijer and Cedric Ryngaert, 'Reflections on *Jaloud v The Netherlands:* Jurisdictional Consequences and Resonance in Dutch Society' (2015) 19(1-2) Journal of International Peacekeeping 174, 180-181.
[15] Milanovic, 54-55; McGoldrick, 71.

respondent state and the applicant, by considering itself incompetent to review a state's military conduct—under an international legal act (i.e. a UN SC resolution), or attributing the state's (mis)conduct to an international organisation (i.e. the UN and/or NATO) covered by immunity—as was the case in *Behrami.*[16] By focusing on responsibility, *Jaloud* essentially demonstrates that states sending troops abroad, in the context of multinational military operations, cannot disregard their Convention obligations—especially since they 'invariably retain ultimate military authority' over their own troops.[17]

Still, it is uncertain whether *Jaloud's* new test for extraterritorial jurisdiction would also apply to foot patrols (which also lack permanence) in future military, or law-enforcement operations abroad.[18] Also interesting to note is whether the previously opposed 'cause-and-effect' notion of jurisdiction has now been abandoned in favour of this new 'checkpoint jurisdiction'.[19] Notably, it is now sufficient to demonstrate that the targeted individual fell under the state's 'checkpoint jurisdiction'—when the state exercises control and authority—by controlling the checkpoint; even if there is an absence of effective overall territorial control. For example, if a state exercises control and authority over its own agents, who, in turn, perform patrolling duties in a foreign territory, anyone who is targeted by those state agents can be brought within the jurisdiction of the relevant state—without the need for the individual to be detained or arrested first. Therefore, the reasoning in *Jaloud* leaves the door open for establishing the ECHR States' jurisdiction in aerial bombardments (previously rejected in *Bankovic*) or targeted killings by drones in future operations. A broader interpretation of *Jaloud* could suggest that the power to target (and kill) an individual, equates to exercising 'physical power and control' over them.[20]

---

[16] See n 9 above.

[17] Aurel Sari, 'Jaloud v Netherlands: New Directions in Extra-Territorial Military Operations' (*EJIL:Talk!* , 24 November 2014) <http://www.ejiltalk.org/jaloud-v-netherlands-new-directions-in-extra-territorial-military-operations/> accessed 05 May 2016, citing Fleck and Gill (eds) *The Handbook of the International Law of Military Operations* (OUP 2011) 237.

[18] Ibid.

[19] See n 10.

[20] Haijer and Ryngaert, 180-181. See also, Marko Milanovic, 'Al-Skeini and Al-Jedda in Strasbourg' (2012) 23(1) EJIL 121, 129.

3. Recent Developments in National Courts

In last year's case of *Al-Saadoon,*[21] the UK High Court was concerned with whether the death of an Iraqi civilian caused by a British soldier during the post-occupation period in Iraq engaged the jurisdiction of the UK for the purposes of Article 1 ECHR. The Court held that, although full sovereignty had passed to the interim Iraqi government—and the UK was no longer exercising public powers—UK forces were still capable of exercising some public powers; including combat operations against insurgents. Therefore, following *Al-Skeini,* the jurisdiction of the UK could be established.[22] Currently, it is also important to identify how the Court found that the individual concerned fell within the jurisdiction of the UK, without being arrested or detained first.

Legatt J, in establishing that a state has exercised 'physical power and control' over an individual, appeared to expand the ECHR's jurisprudence, on the extraterritoriality of the Convention and went further than the Strasbourg Court had previously gone. After carefully considering the Strasbourg case law on the matter, Legatt J concluded that the jurisdiction of the respondent state did apply:

> …in those test cases where the individual was shot by a British soldier both (a) because such shootings occurred in the course of security operations in which British forces were exercising public powers that would normally be exercised by the government of Iraq and (b) because shooting someone involves the exercise of physical power over that person.[23]

By holding that the shooting was an exercise of physical power and control which could bring the individual within the jurisdiction of the UK, Legatt J significantly expanded the existing jurisprudence of the ECHR, which is articulated through the judgment in *Jaloud*. Particular emphasis should also be given to the re-introduction of the 'cause and effect' approach to the jurisdiction that was expressly rejected in *Bankovic.*[24] This reasoning can arguably constitute a game changer in the light of the use of targeted drone attacks, which have become common in modern warfare.

---

[21] *Al-Saadoon & Others v. Secretary of State for Defence* [2015] EWHC 715 (Admin).
[22] Ibid., para 84-86 citing *Al-Skeini*, para 135.
[23] *Al-Saadoon*, para 294.
[24] *Bankovic*, para 75.

4. Drone Strikes and the Concept of 'Physical Power and Control'

The use of a targeted drone strike arguably falls at the extreme end of the spectrum of extraterritorial jurisdiction. Jurisdiction in these situations cannot be established under the territorial principle. Similarly, due to the nature of such drone operations, engaging a state's jurisdiction based on 'effective control over the area' can be considered impossible. However, by presuming that drone strikes produce the same effect as targeting and shooting individuals on the ground, there could be a plausible, and legal basis to establish the element of 'physical power and control'; and ultimately, engage the application of the Convention in such scenarios.

As Legatt J held in *Al-Saadoon*,

> 'it [is] impossible to say that shooting someone dead does not involve the exercise of physical power and control over that person. Using force to kill is indeed the ultimate exercise of physical control over another human being'.[25]

The UK Government argued that, in establishing authority and control of a state, a rational distinction should be maintained between cases where the individual is taken into custody by state agents, and cases where they are not. Legatt J rejected this argument, by stating that 'if the person holding the gun is in such control of the situation that he is able to hold the gun to the individual's head, it may be that the individual is in fact detained'[26]. Adding to this reasoning, it was also pointed out that 'making the applicability of a system of human rights law depends on the distance between the gun and the person's head in a case where a person is shot is not a position which [...] can reasonably be sustained'.[27]

Although references to detainment, or 'gun to the individual's head' may create a presumption that the physical presence of a soldier is a requisite, in establishing a state's physical power and control over an individual, the renaissance of the 'cause and effect' approach to jurisdiction signals an important change in the context of the extraterritoriality of human rights treaties. Indeed, Legatt J's latter statement about the irrelevance of the distance between the soldier and the victim—for the application of the

[25] *Al-Saadoon*, para 95.
[26] Ibid., para 93-94, 96.
[27] Ibid., para 96.

Convention—leaves the door wide-open for engaging a state's jurisdiction, in the context of targeted drone strikes if the concept of 'physical power and control' is established. It is also worth noting that aerial vehicles (e.g. drones) may perform patrol or control duties, over the airspace of a foreign state; either within the context of multinational military operations or assigned to individual state(s). Since such aerial patrols and checkpoints are not permanent establishments—by means of which the state does not exercise effective territorial control—their factual characteristics are significantly similar to the 'normal' checkpoints on the ground (temporary in nature and limited in space). Therefore, one could argue that *Jaloud's* 'checkpoint' test for jurisdiction may also be established in situations of aerial patrols, and checkpoint; engaging states' responsibility, under the ECHR, when individuals are injured by drone attacks.[28]

5. CONCLUSION

In *Jaloud,* the ECHR was presented with some significant legal difficulties in protecting the right to life, in the context of military operations on foreign soil. Apart from the speculations which have come through the re-examination of the concepts of state responsibility, and jurisdiction for the purposes of the application of the ECHR, the Strasbourg Court created the new 'checkpoint' test for the jurisdiction that significantly expanded the scope of extraterritorial application of the ECHR. This expanded notion of jurisdiction has already found application before national courts, where the particular emphasis has been given on the concept of 'physical power and control'. Arguably, this developing jurisprudence on the matter opens new paths for establishing a state's jurisdiction in the light of targeted drone strikes (something which has been generally rejected in previous cases). As the legal basis for such claims gains weight, it should not be surprising to see the courts deciding on cases which have so far been viewed as inadmissible.

---

[28] Haijer and Ryngaert, 180-181.

www.ingramcontent.com/pod-product-compliance
Lightning Source LLC
LaVergne TN
LVHW082349200926
848481LV00012B/3501
* 9 7 9 8 2 1 5 5 8 9 8 3 0 *